Henry VIII and the English Reformation

IN THE SAME SERIES

General Editors: Eric J. Evans and P.D. King

LANCASTER PAMPHLETS

Henry VIII and the English Reformation

D.G. Newcombe

London and New York

To my parents

First published 1995
by Routledge
11 New Fetter Lane, London EC4P 4EE

Simultaneously published in the USA and Canada
by Routledge
29 West 35th Street, New York, NY 10001

Reprinted 2003

Routledge is an imprint of the Taylor & Francis Group

Typeset in Bembo by
Ponting–Green Publishing Services, Chesham, Bucks
Printed and bound in Great Britain by
TJ International Ltd, Padstow, Cornwall

British Library Cataloguing in Publication Data
A catalogue record for this book is available from the British Library

Library of Congress Cataloging in Publication Data
Newcombe, D.G. (David Gordon)
Henry VIII and the English Reformation / D.G. Newcombe.
p.   cm. – (Lancaster pamphlets)
Includes bibliographical references.
1. Great Britain–History–Henry VIII, 1509–1547.
2. Henry VIII, King of England, 1491–1547.
3. England–Church history–16th century.
4. Reformation–England   I. Title.   II. Title: Henry
Eighth and the English Reformation.   III. Series.
DA332.N49   1995
942.03'4–dc20   94–39263

ISBN 0–415–10728–8

Contents

Chronology

1489

March   Treaty of Medina del Campo.

1491

June   Henry Tudor born.

1501

November   Marriage of Arthur Tudor and Catherine of Aragon.

1502

April   Arthur Tudor dies.

1505

March   Julius II grants the dispensation for Henry to marry Catherine.

1509

April   Henry VIII succeeds to the English throne.

June   Marriage of Henry Tudor and Catherine of Aragon.

1512

February   War with France and Scotland.
           Wolsey comes to prominence.

1513

August   The battle of the Spurs.

1517

           Luther publishes the 95 Theses.

1524		
		Tyndale goes into exile.
1525		
	February	French defeated at Pavia by imperial forces.
		Tyndale's translation of the Bible printed.
1527		
	May	Charles V sacks Rome.
	June	Henry VIII decides his marriage is unlawful.
1528		
	October	Cardinal Campeggio arrives in England.
1529		
	May	Hearings open in London to determine the validity of Henry's marriage.
	June	The battle of Landriano and the treaty of Barcelona.
	July	Hearings adjourned in London.
	November	The Reformation Parliament convenes and passes acts against probate, mortuary fees and non-residence.
1530		
	November	Death of Wolsey.
	December	The clergy charged with Praemunire.
1532		
	March	Supplication against the Ordinaries.
	May	Submission of the clergy; resignation of Thomas More from the chancellorship; first Act of Annates.
1533		
	January	Henry secretly marries Anne Boleyn.
	March	Act in Restraint of Appeals.
	May	Cranmer declares Henry's first marriage void.
	September	Elizabeth is born.
1534		
	March	Second Act of Annates; Act of Succession; Treason Act.
	December	Act of Supremacy; Act of First-Fruits and Tenths.
1535		
	June	Fisher executed.
	July	More executed.

1536

January	Catherine of Aragon dies.
April	Statute of Uses; dissolution of the lesser monasteries.
May	Anne Boleyn executed; Henry marries Jane Seymour.
July	Publication of the Ten Articles.
August	Injunctions of 1536.
October	The Pilgrimage of Grace begins.
December	The Pilgrimage of Grace ends.

1537

October	Edward is born; death of Jane Seymour; Matthew Bible issued; the 'Bishop's Book' published.

1538

September	Injunctions of 1538.

1539

April	Act of Six Articles.

1540

January	Henry marries Anne of Cleves.
July	The marriage is annulled; Cromwell executed; Henry marries Catherine Howard.

1542

February	Catherine Howard executed.
October	War with Scotland.

1543

July	Henry marries Catherine Parr.
May	The 'King's Book' published. Act for the Advancement of True Religion. Attempts to remove Cranmer fail.

1544

July	War in France. Attempts to discredit Gardiner fail.

1545

November	Henry makes a plea for tolerance in religion.

1546

December	Norfolk arrested for treason.

1547

January	Henry VIII dies.

Glossary

benefit of clergy	the exemption of clergy from trial by a secular court. This privilege was extended to all orders of clergy and to nuns. By the sixteenth century the exemption usually only applied to a *first* felonious offence.
chantries	a benefice maintained to say the Mass for the benefit of souls, specifically the soul of the founder but possibly including others. Usually a chantry was a chapel or altar located in a larger church or cathedral building, but many examples exist of detached chapels built specifically as chantries. They were particularly popular in the fourteenth and fifteenth centuries.
confraternities and religious guilds	associations formed to pray for the souls of members who had died and to make provision for their funerals. They did have other religious roles, such as the maintenance of shrines. Some even founded schools or made arrangements for members who were in financial difficulty.
indulgences	the remission, by the Church, of punishment due to sin. The Church assumed that all sin was punished either on earth or in

	purgatory. Christ and the saints, however, had built up a 'treasury of merit' in heaven which the Church could draw upon in consideration of the good works of any individual. The system was abused widely.
Lollards	followers of John Wyclif. Probably meaning 'mumblers of prayers', the term came to be loosely applied to those suspected of heresy, dissatisfied with the Church or disputing tithes.
mortuary fees	fees payable to the clergy for burial in consecrated ground.
nepotism	the granting of a benefice or ecclesiastical office to a relative.
non-residence	continual absence from a benefice lawfully held.
Ordinaries	all clergymen who had the authority to exercise jurisdiction. This jurisdiction included teaching, governing, adjudicating, and the administration of the sacraments.
pilgrimages	journeys to holy places. They were undertaken as acts of devotion, penance or in search of miraculous cures. Jerusalem was one popular pilgrimage destination, as was the tomb of St Thomas Becket at Canterbury.
pluralism	the holding of more than one benefice at the same time.
Praemunire	the statutes of 1353, 1365 and 1393 were all referred to by this title. They were designed to protect the English Crown against jurisdictional encroachments by the papacy. Appeals from English courts to Rome were forbidden, and the promulgation of papal bulls and excommunications was also proscribed.
probate fees	fees charged for the proving and administration of wills.
Provisors	passed in 1351, this statute prohibited the Pope from presenting any benefices in England.

purgatory	a place of punishment where those who have died with some sins unforgiven must go until they have done sufficient penance. Once they have endured their punishment, they are permitted to enter heaven. Purgatory is like hell but not eternal.
simony	the buying or selling of Church offices or other spiritual things.
tithe	the tenth part of all produce from the land, labour and livestock to each clergyman serving a parish for his maintenance. Calculations of what was owed as a tithe were the subject of continuous dispute.

Introduction

When Henry VIII died on 28 January 1547, he left behind him a Church in England that was in transition. It had left the obedience of the Church of Rome and, however much the English Church may have considered itself part of the universal Church, Rome considered it schismatic. It no longer looked to the Pope as the supreme head – now that role had been assumed by the king. But it was only in throwing off the authority of the Pope that the Church in England bore any resemblance to the Protestant Churches on the continent. There were few doctrinal changes of any significance. The rejection of papal authority and the adjustment of ecclesiastical administration that resulted while an essentially orthodox structure of belief was maintained made the Church in England unique. This was entirely due to the particular needs and tempestuous leadership of Henry VIII. The king was not a Protestant and did not want a Protestant Church in England, but a break with Rome had served his political and dynastic purposes. In 1547, the government of the new king, Edward VI, and the episcopal leadership of the Church were prepared and willing to go much further down the Protestant path in practical and doctrinal terms than had ever been envisaged by the monarch who started it all, for Henry remained orthodox in his theology to the end. If the Church was not Protestant on 28 January 1547, it was about to become so.

Of course, the Church in 1547 did not look Protestant. Few

1

people would have noticed many changes in the day-to-day practice of their religion. It is true that by that date the monasteries had been dissolved and the Pope had been removed from the prayers that were recited at services of worship, but the Mass was retained, as were most of the beliefs and ceremonies that had come to be such important parts of the lives of local parishioners. This presented quite a different picture from that created by the radical changes that had taken place on the continent. The Reformation in England during the time of Henry VIII was different: it was different in its motivation; it was different in the methods used to achieve its ends; and it was different in its immediate result.

As a result, any study of the Reformation in England is plagued with confusion and unexpected paradoxes. Modern methods of research into the period, using not only surviving chronicles, letters, sermons and propaganda but also official government documents, private wills and diocesan and parish registers, have shed some light but often served only to confuse matters. Were abuses widespread or were they not, for instance? The evidence is not clear. Were the clergy respected, despised or tolerated by the people? It is difficult to know. What people thought is just as important as what the evidence shows, and yet knowing what ordinary folk thought presents enormous problems. In fact, we will probably never really know. What we do know, however, is this: the traditional Protestant interpretation of an old and decrepit Church, riddled with abuses of all kinds and controlled by an Italian princeling whose only concern was to sap England's wealth for his own temporal ambitions, is no longer viable. What is more, any notion that Protestantism swept to prominence in England on the crest of a great wave of popular revulsion against the old Church does not stand up to close scrutiny.

The Reformation in Henry VIII's time was an enormously complex process. It was complicated by the fact that so many of the changes that were made were wrought in the political not the ecclesiastical arena. The government and Parliament had the initiative, not the Church. The historian Maurice Powicke's famous observation that the English Reformation was an act of state rather than an act of faith has been embedded in the minds of all students of the period but it bears repeating. Powicke was not the first to notice this: the Protestant historian John Foxe, whose descriptions of the events of the Reformation in England were so instrumental in forming the traditional picture of what happened, was convinced that Henry VIII had no real intention of reforming the Church, but rather intended only to secure the succession by a divorce which he could only ensure if he controlled the necessary machinery of the Church in England.[1] The actual transformation that took place later, from Catholic to Protestant, may seem almost an accidental or incidental by-product of what was essentially a political solution to a dynastic problem. The political solution is rather easier to define than the religious change. While statutes may be passed in an instant, beliefs change much more slowly.

What complicates all of this is that there was a significant minority of people in England who were influenced by the process of reform that was occurring elsewhere. On the continent, from Martin Luther's protest of 1517 onwards, challenges were being thrown down to the Church of Rome, its doctrine and its practice. The Church had been challenged before, as we shall see, but never in so effective or widespread a manner. Owing to the many contacts that sixteenth-century England had with the continent, politically, intellectually and economically, these challenges were known in England and they influenced politicians, scholars, churchmen and merchants. Indeed, there is evidence that these subversive religious ideas, which would later be called 'Protestant', percolated down into the population. England had its own home-grown variety of heretical opinion in those who followed the teachings of the fourteenth-century Oxford thinker and critic of the Church, John Wyclif, and this minority was especially receptive to Protestant ideas.

But Henry VIII's agenda was quite different and he was generally hostile to the reforming ideas that began to find their way to England from continental Europe. It is best not to forget that it was under Henry's name that a defence of orthodoxy, *Assertio septem sacramentorum adversus Martinum Lutherum* (Defence of the Seven Sacraments against Martin Luther), was published in 1521 and earned him the title 'Defender of the Faith'. This papal recognition pleased Henry and he kept it in his royal style even after the break with Rome. Indeed, there is little evidence to suggest that Henry was dissatisfied with the doctrines or practices of the Church in themselves. Yet he was not above using the ideas of the continental reformers when it suited him, and he sent out such mixed signals that Luther's right-hand man, Philip Melanchthon, dedicated one of his most important theological works to none other than Henry VIII: the same Henry VIII who had so violently attacked Lutheran doctrine in 1521.

If this appears confusing now, imagine how confusing it was for people at the time. In the first flush of excitement after the break with Rome, many changes were mooted: a Bible and services in the vernacular, and an end to the celibacy of the clergy, to name but two. Yet the king was never comfortable with most of these 'reforms' and was easily persuaded to revert to orthodoxy when he felt that things had gone too far or when those factions that resisted radical reform were in favour at court. Those who saw the king as a Protestant were sadly mistaken, and some paid for their mistakes with their lives.

The Reformation in England was different, then. Attempting to understand what happened with any clarity is a thorny problem and has often sparked off acrimonious debate among historians. A number of attempts have been made to identify what was different about the English Reformation, and why, and students of the period are to be forgiven if they become confused by the multitude of theories. Although the subject of this pamphlet is the Henrician Reformation, it is worth noting that some of the more sophisticated arguments tend to take the entire sixteenth century into account and often reach well into the seventeenth century for an understanding of the process of Reformation. But most theories have at their heart the notion that it was the reign of Henry VIII that 'got the ball rolling', regardless of when they date the actual conversion of England from a Catholic to a Protestant nation.

In very broad brushstrokes,[2] there are two main schools of thought about the Henrician Reformation. One school, led by Professor Geoffrey Elton, argues that the Reformation in England during the reign of Henry VIII happened quickly and was imposed by the government. According to this analysis, the Reformation was 'official' and depended more on the strength of statutes passed in Parliament than on any evangelical efforts made by the reformers. As it was imposed from above, the actual business of changing what people believed was less important than conformity to the law. Enforcement at a local level was therefore important. This was often difficult: some areas readily accepted the changes that were made while others, most notably much of the north of England, demonstrated strong resistance. The key point in this argument, however, is that the Reformation was enacted and enforced by the government.

The second general school of thought was pioneered by the historian A. G. Dickens. He argued, in his groundbreaking study *The English Reformation*, that there was sufficient heterodox opinion in England on the eve of the Reformation to make the transformation from a nominally Catholic nation to a Protestant one rather easier than might have been expected. To one degree or another, the initiative for this change came from the people. Dickens and his disciples point to anticlerical and anti-Catholic sentiment at the grassroots as well as to strong Lollard* influences. He notes the growing influence of Lollardy among merchants and artisans and the evidence of heterodoxy at a local level being dealt with in the Church courts. According to this view, the Reformation in England went as far as it did with the speed that it did because of support from the people. The Reformation was fast and from below.

Neither of these views is entirely satisfactory. On the one hand, Elton and his school have been accused of undervaluing the problems that the government had in the enforcement of the official Reformation. Dickens, on the other hand, appears to give too much weight to the Lollards and to the existence of heterodox opinion in England generally. What the two have in common is the idea that it all happened quickly and clearly. From a strictly legal standpoint, as we have seen, this may be true, but sufficient evidence exists to make us doubt how quickly and clearly the Reformation won the hearts and minds of the people. Some historians, notably Professor Patrick Collinson, have taken a longer view of the changes and, while admitting that the 'official Reformation' took place very quickly indeed, have maintained that the process of conversion took rather longer and may not have even begun until the reign of Elizabeth.

The very fact that the Reformation in England looked so different from what occurred elsewhere has prompted some historians to question the validity of the very concept of a single, unified event called 'the Reformation'. Christopher Haigh has argued that there were several reformations during the sixteenth century and that only one of these was evangelical in nature, the rest being purely political.[3] This represents what he refers to as a 'deconstructed' view. Yet it is hard to separate out the issues in this way. The move towards religious reform was part and parcel of the political reform that was going on at the same time, and each supported and informed the other. It is certainly hard to see that the issues were separated at the time.

The Reformation in the time of Henry VIII was motivated by the desire of the king to secure the succession of the Tudor dynasty in England. When the normal means of achieving his ends were exhausted without a positive result, Henry set about reaching his goal by using, encouraging and, perhaps, amplifying critical religious sentiment and even what had previously been considered heretical opinions. In doing so, he let the genie out of the bottle. What had been a minority opinion was given a much more powerful voice than it would otherwise have had because of the difficulties the king was having with an uncooperative Pope. Any description of the Henrician Reformation must begin with an examination of the state of the Church before the process that led to the break with Rome and, ultimately, doctrinal change.

1

Why a Reformation?

The Church, like most institutions, is always in need of reformation; in fact, it is a sign of health when it recognises the need and acts to renew itself. Throughout its history, it has frequently undergone massive internal change in order to meet the challenges that new times and ideas have thrown down to it. One need only reflect for a moment on how St Francis introduced a new dimension to the ministry of the Church through his reforming movement in the thirteenth century, to see how this reform within the Church was both possible and desirable. Popes, too, far from always being resistant to change, were frequently responsible for re-ordering, rationalising and reforming the Church in order to minister more effectively in changing times and circumstances. Reform and reformation did not necessarily imply the destruction of the Church, its forms of worship or its structure. It did mean growth, albeit sometimes painful.

If, however, we use the term 'Reformation', we are not referring to the normal process of renewal that the Church had engaged in for centuries. As a technical term, 'Reformation' applies to the great social and religious upheaval that occurred mainly in the sixteenth century. Of course, most people interested in radical change would not have seen themselves as attempting to introduce anything new or innovative – far from it. Rather they believed they were restoring the Church to what they considered to be its former purity. Just when that time of the pure Church existed was open to debate and there were many different opinions. For some, like the radical Protestant bishop of Gloucester, John Hooper (*c*. 1495–1555), the Church may have lost its purity after the martyrdom of St Polycarp (second century AD); others tended to date the decline of the Church much later, perhaps six hundred or even a thousand years after Christ. What they all had in common was a vision of the purity of the primitive Church and a determination to re-establish its practices and theology as they understood them. As far as they were concerned, the papacy and the Church of Rome had polluted that purity with false and invented doctrines. The Church needed cleansing to return it to purity. Their critique of the Church, therefore, concentrated not only on the abuses that many perceived among the clergy but also included the doctrine of the Church, which they felt had gone seriously astray.

For our purposes, then, the term 'Reformation' has a very particular meaning. It is applied to those events, religious, social and political, which appear to have occurred in relation to a shift away from the traditional Catholicism of the Church of Rome, its theology, discipline and spirituality, and towards those ideas, innovations and forms of worship which have come to be known as Protestant. But the term 'Protestant' itself was not in common usage during the sixteenth century except in very specific circumstances and is a term applied by historians to those of particular religious points of view.[1] What is indisputable is that something happened in sixteenth-century Europe on a grand scale. Part event, part process, it involved an enormous range of disparate elements: social, economic, even technological changes came into play. Beginning with Martin Luther, although with antecedents in the fourteenth century, like Wyclif in England, or in the fifteenth century, like Jan Hus in Bohemia, it swept through Europe like wildfire and touched the lives of most people one way or another. Some it consumed, others it strengthened; all it influenced.

How far had this Reformation touched England before Henry VIII broke with Rome? The answer to this question is enormously complex, in large part because of the complicated motives behind the move to reform in the first place. As we have noted, the Reformation in England was different. There appeared to be no compelling reason to move away from the

8

Church of Rome. There seems to have been general satisfaction with the way the Church operated, and the number of dissidents was small. In addition, the process of internal reform was not being neglected. Where problems were found they were dealt with, and structures to make reform possible existed. Diocesan bishops were often engaged in the business of looking after the pastoral needs of their dioceses, while John Morton, archbishop of Canterbury from 1486 to 1500, had been notable in his efforts to correct abuses he found among the lower orders of the clergy and to curb the excesses of some of the monastic houses.

Still, dissatisfaction did exist. In large part this was because abuses were only the tip of the iceberg. There were always those who were jealous of the wealth of the Church and who sought to turn that wealth to their own use. There were also those who resented the influence of the Church courts and desired to bring more, if not all, legal questions under the jurisdiction of the Common Law courts. These resentments were nothing new. But there was emerging in England a more serious challenge to the Church, with which its normal disciplinary structures could not cope. Whereas Archbishop Morton might believe it necessary to prune a few branches from an essentially healthy tree, there were some for whom the trunk was rotten. Abuses among the clergy were acknowledged by everyone to one degree or another, but for some they were symptomatic of a much deeper ill. If, for instance, spurious pardons were being sold, or indulgences* preached using questionable methods, then perhaps this reflected a serious defect in the Church's traditional understanding of the doctrine of salvation, not simply the problem of a few unscrupulous pardoners. If the clergy were guilty of having mistresses in spite of their vows, then the problem might lie in the requirement of celibacy.

More dangerous still was the reliance of these challengers on Scripture as the final authority and their consequent denial of the authority of the Church and the Pope. As Professor Guy points out, William Tyndale's development of 'the ideas "Truth as revealed in Scripture" and "We must rather obey God than men"' became essential to the defence of the king's position in the 1530s.[2] This point brought the ideas of the reformers and of the king into a strange and often uncomfortable conjunction: despite the usefulness of his ideas, Tyndale was forced into exile – just

9

as the king was about to embark on a serious challenge to ecclesiastical authority. Orthodox on most theological matters, the king found these heterodox ideas useful.

Who were the early reformers in England?

As yet in England there were few who looked beyond the correction of abuses and wanted a complete overhaul of the doctrine of the Church. Typical of the kind of reforming spirit in the early sixteenth century were men like Thomas More, the lawyer and future chancellor, and John Colet, dean of St Paul's. Heavily influenced by the humanism of Desiderius Erasmus, men such as these were not afraid to criticise the Church but were intent on remaining within it.[3] The humanism or 'New Learning' that Erasmus championed built upon a revival of the study of pagan, classical writers and a deep textual criticism. Erasmus, while publishing a number of satirical works which were sharply critical of the clergy and the Church, made his most significant contribution in a new translation of the New Testament. Returning to the original Greek texts, his version was more accurate than that commonly used, the Vulgate, and his corrections served 'to undermine the scriptural authority of the priesthood and the papacy'.[4] Armed with new critical tools, humanists in England attempted to revitalise the Church.

More's great work *Utopia* satirised contemporary Christian values by imagining a society which was essentially humane yet not Christian. His ironic point was that this imaginary, pagan society was superior to, and had much to teach, sixteenth-century Christian European society. While More's subtlety was not lost on his readers, John Colet took a more direct approach. Invited to preach before the Convocation of Canterbury in 1511, Colet was scathing in his criticism of the clergy and of the bishops. The clergy were guilty of worldliness, lust, greed and ambition, and the bishops, who ought to have been attempting to rectify these problems, were setting poor examples themselves. These attacks were not welcomed by the ecclesiastical establishment, but it was always clear that neither Colet nor More desired to do any more than reform the existing structure from within it. Colet was never a 'Protestant', and More became the scourge of those who challenged the doctrine of the

Church. However uncomfortable the humanist critique may have been for the leaders of the Church, the followers of this 'New Learning' were not heretics.

As noted earlier, England had its own tradition of heretical teachings. John Wyclif had first advanced his ideas at Oxford towards the end of the fourteenth century. That was a time when confidence in the Church was at a very low ebb: the papacy had earlier moved from Rome to Avignon (prompting English suspicions that the Pope was no more than a French chaplain),[5] and there were at one time three separate and competing popes.[6] Wyclif's teachings had called for a Bible in English and the dissolution of monasteries, had attacked Church property and had argued for a rolling-back of priestly and papal power. He also had a vision of 'a new order of society . . . in which citizens obeyed the lay prince as priest and king'.[7] In fact, Wyclif's programme for reform anticipated many of the criticisms that reformers in the sixteenth century were to level at the Church.

However, Wyclif's reforms, although interesting to the powerful John of Gaunt, who became his protector, were never instituted, not least because the English government in the late fourteenth century was unstable enough as it was without embarking on so ambitious a project as Wyclif proposed. The support that he had among the nobility and middle classes gave his ideas a certain respectability until they became associated with the rebellion of Sir John Oldcastle in 1414. Wyclif's followers now began to be persecuted and were forced underground. There they remained, known as Lollards, only surfacing periodically to be tried for heresy.

How extensive a community the Lollards were in the sixteenth century is a matter open to question. By the eve of the Reformation they appear to have existed in some regions of the country primarily among the merchant and artisan classes. The complicated and elegant ideas of John Wyclif had degenerated somewhat over the course of a century into a very simplistic attack on ceremony, the veneration of images, belief in purgatory, and priests, and the identifying badge of Lollardy was the translation of the Bible into English known as the 'Lollard Bible'. Lollardy seems to have been largely a phenomenon of southern England. London, Essex and Kent in particular appear to have had strong Lollard communities. Bristol in the south-west and Coventry in the Midlands were also centres of Lollard support. However, the Lollards were hardly representative of common public opinion, and whether Lollardy provided any real leadership in the Protestant cause is debatable. In fact, it has been argued that Lollards and Protestants did not always consider themselves fellow travellers.[8] However, there were those in England who took matters a step further than either the Lollards or the humanists.

In the early part of the sixteenth century a new breed of reformed thinker was emerging. It must be stressed that they were few, and it is as a result of the ultimate victory of Protestantism over Catholicism in England that these early reformers have been given the prominence by historians that they have received. At the time, they were on the margins, even if their attacks did sometimes provoke responses from the highest levels of government.

The centre for this group of reformers was Cambridge, its leader the Augustinian prior Robert Barnes. Barnes was an intelligent and vocal critic of the clergy and the bishops and, although forced to recant his views in the 1520s, continued as an important voice for reform under the protection of Thomas Cromwell until 1540. Barnes and his followers initially gathered at the White Horse Tavern, where they discussed, and were influenced by, the writings of Martin Luther and other continental reformers. From this group would emerge two of the future leaders of the Church in England: Thomas Cranmer and Hugh Latimer.

Perhaps the best known of these new Protestants was William Tyndale, because he published his criticisms and his English translation of the New Testament. Horrified by what he saw as the ignorance of the clergy, particularly in his West Country home, and influenced by the writings of Luther on salvation, Tyndale began a campaign of criticism which attracted followers in the 1520s. He was persuaded by the Lutheran concept of salvation by faith alone and, as a consequence, attacked the doctrine of purgatory and the practice of indulgences. More than that, he developed a political theology that challenged the power of the priesthood and vested the power to reform the Church in the king, who, after all, was chosen by God to govern. Although these opinions, and especially Tyndale's antagonism towards the papal authority, were attractive to a king who wished to challenge that authority, there was no question but that Tyndale's opinions were considered heretical, especially after the publication of his translation of the New Testament in 1525. It was Tyndale's most important contribution to the Reformation. This Bible in English, based on Erasmus' translation from the Greek, added much that was antipapal and anticlerical in the margins, although the translation itself was faithful. In 1524, he was forced to flee to the continent, where he carried on a violent pamphlet battle with Thomas More until he was captured and executed for heresy by the forces of the Holy Roman Emperor Charles V in 1536. In Tyndale's thinking, the ideas of the Lollards and humanism amalgamated and grew. His reliance on Scripture as the final and most important authority made him uncompromising in his positions. Therefore, although his opinions on the authority of the Pope were much to the liking of Henry VIII, he was unable to support the king's wishes for a divorce because he could find no Scriptural justification for it.

The issues were not raised by Tyndale alone. Others, such as Thomas Bilney, Thomas Arthur and John Frith, found themselves in trouble with the authorities for their outspoken opinions. Frith, a devoted disciple of Tyndale, was expelled from Oxford for his views and fled to the continent in 1528 to join his mentor. Returning to England to organise support for the Protestant cause, he was captured and burned at the stake in 1533. Bilney and Arthur were both tried for heresy at Cambridge in 1527. While Arthur, who had criticised ecclesiastical jurisdiction, admitted his error, Bilney proved a much more difficult case. On most matters very orthodox, indeed hardly a Protestant at all, he was outspoken in his opposition to the veneration of images, which he deemed idolatry, and to papal pardons on the grounds that these seemed to denigrate the sufficiency of Christ in the matter of salvation. Was Christ's sacrifice on the cross not enough to ensure forgiveness of sins? Recognising his peril, Bilney managed to answer carefully the questions put to him, but in the end was forced into a humiliating recantation. The recantation was half-hearted, however. Soon thereafter Bilney was distributing Protestant books and preaching without a licence in Norfolk. For this he was burned at the stake in 1531 and was immortalised by Protestant historians (most notably John Foxe) as a martyr to a cause to which he was only ever marginally committed.

The importance of these early reformers was inflated later by Protestant historians. The reformers reached only a small percentage of the population and, as often as not, preached to the already converted or the disaffected. They were primarily influential among the young scholars at Cambridge during the halcyon days of the White Horse Tavern. Important though their influence was among the future leaders of the Church of England, they were not particularly influential with the general population.

What were the issues?

Just as the newly formed Parliament of 1529 was about to meet, a Protestant firebrand, Simon Fish, published his tract *A Supplication of Beggars*. He painted a dismal picture of the clergy and the state of the Church, as did his fellow common lawyer, Christopher St German, who built a case against the clergy by listing known examples of clerical abuse. We have already noted John Colet's criticism of the clergy in 1511. All these have been seen as evidence of the reality of violent anticlerical sentiment in England and the abuses that were laid at the door of the clergy.

But what were those abuses, and what were the issues that the reformers focused on in their attack on the Church? There were two levels of criticism directed at the Church. First, there was criticism of abuses of practice – aspects of Church discipline which were violated and either ignored or not dealt with effectively by the existing structures within the institution. Second, there was criticism of practices which the reformers felt to be intrinsically wrong – ceremonies, traditions, and 'superstitions' based on an incorrect analysis of Scripture or a faulty theological interpretation. While Thomas More or John Colet might agree that there were problems of discipline that cried out for reform, they would not agree that the theology of the Church was in error.

The problems that existed in ecclesiastical discipline in the early sixteenth century were nothing new. The Church had been wrestling with these persistent breaches of discipline for centuries: sometimes effectively, sometimes not. The abuses most commonly cited were simony,* pluralism,* non-residence,* nepotism,* sexual misconduct, ignorance and benefit of clergy.*

All of these had been recognised as abuses from very early on and for good reason. Often used as a means of unfair advancement in the Church, simony had been outlawed by early councils of the Church, but it proved very difficult to control. Pluralism was frowned upon because it meant that some parishes might be neglected by clergy who were busy elsewhere. However, one benefice might not produce sufficient income for the clergyman's support, and so dispensations were granted by Rome if this was the case. Assurances were required that all parishes would be looked after adequately by curates, but there were abuses of this system: some clergy held more than two benefices, some bishops held more than one diocese. The curates hired by pluralists were not usually of the best quality; as they were paid only a small percentage of the income of the parish, such a position was not attractive to the best candidates. In some cases, no curate was provided at all. The main complaint was that the people of the parish were not being served adequately.

Non-residence might be the result of pluralism, but a more common cause was that the priest might be employed elsewhere. It was not uncommon for the clergy to serve as stewards, managing the estates or affairs of the wealthy. In addition, the clergy often served the government in a variety of positions which drew them away from their parishes or dioceses on a regular or even permanent basis. Even a casual glance at the men who served Henry VIII as diplomats reveals that many were either bishops or priests. If they were conscientious, they left men adequate to look after their cures but sometimes this did not happen. Again, those who suffered were the people whose spiritual needs the Church existed to serve.

The more powerful among the clergy were often guilty of nepotism as they often had a number of benefices at their disposal to dispense as they saw fit. (Thomas Cardinal Wolsey, chancellor of England and archbishop of York, for instance, secured benefices for his son Thomas Winter even though Winter was studying in Paris.) As a consequence, nepotism was followed by non-residency and, because one benefice was often not enough to provide a comfortable living, by pluralism.[9]

Sexual misconduct was simply that: the clergy had all taken a vow of celibacy and were not supposed to have sexual relations of any kind. By the sixteenth century clerical celibacy had been in force for some five hundred years, although it had not always been part of the tradition of the Church. Sometimes local custom accepted clergy who had female companions and even families, despite the overall ban on such behaviour. The bulk of sexual charges (and there were few of these) brought against the clergy had to do with behaviour far more scandalous than simple cohabitation.

Ignorance was a charge which was made especially against the poorer clergy who served as curates in parishes held in plurality. While some of the clergy had university education, a great number had only rudimentary training. The issue was not whether the clergy were highly educated but whether, in some cases, they were able to read the services and understand them. After the break with Rome, it was discovered in Gloucester that ten of the clergy could not recite the Lord's Prayer. This was taken as an indication of how badly standards had slipped in the pre-Reformation Church. Charges of ignorance raised real questions about the ability of the clergy to perform their parochial function.

Originally designed to protect the clergy and extended even to the minor orders, benefit of clergy was a privilege where the opportunities for abuse were plentiful. The Church had recognised this and took steps to curtail abuses – even going so far as to brand the hands of those who had claimed benefit of clergy and were not entitled to do so again. But the apparent injustice of this privilege could still provoke anger among the laity. In 1514, when the coroner's jury returned a verdict of murder and charged several of the bishop of London's officers after Richard Hunne was found hanged in a cell in the bishop of London's palace, the accused escaped trial by claiming benefit of clergy. London was outraged at the time, and the case had not been forgotten by those who assembled in Parliament in 1529.

In addition to these abuses, there were long-standing grievances to do with the way the Church raised money to maintain its ministry, and the way it administered justice in its courts. The Church raised its money through a tax known as the tithe,* and through fees that it charged for a variety of spiritual services. Refusal to pay could result in arrest and prosecution before the Church courts. Richard Hunne, for instance, found himself in the bishop of London's gaol because he had refused to pay one such fee – the mortuary fee.* Some questioned whether it was possible for the Church to dispense justice fairly where its own financial interests were involved or where its own officials were in jeopardy.

While these issues of practice tended to be eye-catching – everyone understood what the sexual misconduct of the clergy meant – the more specifically theological issues were equally, if not more, important in the debate. Here we find a number of issues which caused serious disagreement. Most of these were based on an understanding of Christian theology which relied on the ultimate authority of Scripture and on the insights of Martin Luther. The central problem was how one could come to eternal life, and the question that the reformers asked was simply: what is necessary for salvation?

Like Luther, they found the answer in the Bible. They argued that only those requirements for eternal life found specifically in Scripture were necessary. Anything else was superfluous, of human invention, or even antithetical to the pursuit of salvation. For some reformers this appeal to Scriptural authority meant that any observance, custom or belief that could not be supported by Scripture was not to be accepted; indeed, acceptance might be harmful to one's spiritual health. Others, like the writer Thomas Starkey, would argue that some of the traditions of the Church, while not being necessary, might be useful to one's spiritual life. This moderate position was not generally shared by radical reformers although the Church of England would ultimately follow the middle way that Starkey first enunciated.

The key to understanding all the issues raised by the early reformers, however, is the doctrine of salvation by faith alone. Once a theologian accepted the notion that there was nothing one could actively do to achieve eternal life except have faith, then the structure that the Church had built around the doctrine of salvation began to crumble. The doctrine of purgatory,* the half-way house between heaven and hell, was objected to as a human invention without Scriptural authority or proof. Indulgences were objected to because they implied that the love of God as demonstrated in the sacrifice of His Son was not enough and that somehow the human agency of the Pope or the Church might have some control over the benefits of God's love. The veneration of the saints, nowhere commanded in the Bible, was seen as denying that Christ himself was sufficient to intercede for our salvation. The veneration of images was seen as idolatrous and completely contrary to Scripture. Pilgrimages* were seen as superstitious and not required of Christians. Finally, transubstantiation, the doctrine that the consecrated bread and wine of the Eucharist actually became the body and blood of Christ (despite their appearance), was attacked as absurd and lacking Scriptural authority.

As the central text on which the reformers based these criticisms was the Bible, the refusal of the English Church to allow the Bible to be published in the vernacular was seen as an attempt by the Church to keep the Christian religion in the hands of the Church and away from the people. Access to this essential Christian text was believed by reformers from Wyclif to Luther to be vitally important to the development of faith. Up to a point, the people were encouraged by the reformers to make up their own minds. While the Bible was available in the vernacular in several countries, the Council of Oxford in 1407, moved by hostility to the Lollard Bible, had outlawed English translations. In fact, parts of the Bible in translation did exist and many reformers included in their tracts large sections of Scripture in translation, but no complete and official version existed. The established Church feared unorthodox interpretations which could lead to heresy, such as Lollardy, and wanted to maintain control of the central text.

The debate over the vernacular Bible, especially when seen from a distance, would seem to be evidence of great dissatisfaction with the Church, but was it? We have already suggested that the traditional view of a decrepit Church riddled with corruption will no longer stand the test of the evidence and we have argued that those who were so vocal in their criticisms were an unrepresentative minority. What was the state of the Church in England in the early sixteenth century? What did the people think?

England and the Church on the eve of the Reformation

John Foxe and many Protestant historians who followed him depicted a Church which was diseased and in need of radical surgery. The Church was corrupt at the top, according to these historians, and the people hated and ridiculed their clergy.

Modern research, however, suggests an alternative view. The Church may not have been in such bad shape after all.

We know that at the beginning of the sixteenth century parishioners continued to support their parish and its needs with their time and treasure. Bequests to local churches and other religious foundations continued unabated. Confraternities and religious guilds,* originally designed to serve the same function for the souls of the less well-off as chantries* did for the wealthy, saw their most popular period during the first quarter of the sixteenth century. What is more, along with their primary function of praying for the souls of the dead thought to be suffering somewhere between heaven and hell, they were expanding their activities to include a wide range of services for the living community. Whatever the reformers might think of the doctrine of purgatory, it was alive and well in early Tudor England, as were traditional ceremonial and piety. One historian has recently noted the enormous popularity of books of traditional devotion well into the 1530s and wonders why, if Catholic Christianity was as displeasing to the general population as the Protestant writers would have us believe, these books went through so many editions.[10] Local traditions and customs, such as observance of saints' days, were also important and helped to define and bring together communities; the great reluctance to give these up was demonstrated later in the 1549 uprisings throughout the West Country, especially in Devon and Cornwall. The people appear to have been, by and large, content with orthodoxy and suspicious of change.

If the people were orthodox, they were certainly encouraged in this by the Crown. All students of medieval English history are familiar with the occasional conflicts between English kings and the Church. The well-known contests between Henry II and Thomas Becket or King John and Pope Innocent III are just two examples of a long-running struggle between the temporal and ecclesiastical powers for jurisdiction and control. But by the fifteenth century that battle had been decided, as a matter of practice, for the Crown. From that time a state of cooperation existed between the English Crown and the papacy despite periodic sabre-rattling and the continued existence in English law of statutes designed to curtail the rights traditionally claimed by the papacy. The Statute of Provisors (1351)* and the Statute of Praemunire (1353)* were both introduced at a time when the papacy had its headquarters at Avignon and when England, at war with France, was suspicious of French influence. Both were intended to prevent papal (and French) interference in English ecclesiastical appointments and legal decisions. These statutes, however, were enforced selectively at the best of times and completely ignored when it was in the best interests of the Crown.

Moreover, since the early years of the fifteenth century, there had existed what might be termed a 'special relationship' between England and Rome. In 1417, on the strength of his brilliant successes against the French on the battlefield, Henry V was in the political ascendancy in Europe. As a result, English delegates to the Council of Constance carried far more weight than was usual and were instrumental in restoring some kind of order to the Church, which had found itself divided by factionalism and by three separate popes competing for the allegiance of all Western Christendom. Pope Martin V, who eventually emerged from the maelstrom, was prepared to grant kings of England powers of patronage and control over the Church such as he granted to no one else. Although English kings had been exercising these powers for some time, this was official recognition, and though future popes may have regretted Martin's generosity and attempted to claw back some of that power, they were never successful.

What is more, the English Crown always did rather well financially out of the Church. The clergy in England had always been taxed heavily – although the convenient fiction had been maintained that the clergy were voluntarily donating money to the Crown – and that burden grew during the reign of Henry VII. Far from preventing Rome from taxing the English people, the Crown usually allowed collection and then skimmed substantial percentages from this revenue for its own use. The papacy, always eager for English support, rarely objected too strenuously. A healthy, wealthy and compliant Church was always in the best interests of the Crown.

In his sermon of 1511, alluded to earlier, John Colet identified the main complaints against the clergy and the bishops. We have looked briefly at all these problems, and the one common theme running through them is that they were thought to get in the way of effective ministry either by bringing the Church into disrepute or by distracting the individual clergyman from his main task, which was, after all, to serve the spiritual needs of those souls in his care. Charges of sexual immorality against the clergy, for instance, always attracted much gossipy attention. Yet, despite several spectacular scandals, there seem to have been relatively few clergy brought to book on charges of this sort. When the evidence is examined carefully, one finds that the same is true of almost all the abuses cited by the reformers – things were not as bad as they claimed them to be. Non-resident clergy were, for the most part, responsible in their appointment of curates. The level of education among the clergy had been rising since the fifteenth century. There were fewer cases of simony and nepotism. The Church courts, in general, were serving justice not with an eye to profit, but with a sensitivity to the pastoral needs of the community.

If the Church was not in desperate need of radical reform, why did it come about? The answer to this question is to be found, first, in the vested interests of the noble and merchant classes, who had much to gain materially if the power and wealth of the Church were broken. These men seized on the polemic of Fish and St German's work as proof of the corruption of the Church. Fish's work was more hyperbolic than realistic, and St German's list of abuses reflected more what was happening on the continent than anything that was true in the English Church. These only served the purposes of those who wished to diminish the Church for their own benefit. The second reason for the Reformation in England, and by far the more important, was to be found in the mind of Henry VIII and his dynastic and political priorities.

2

The 'King's Great Matter'

It was hardly a surprise when, on 23 May 1533 in the archi-episcopal court at Dunstable, Archbishop Thomas Cranmer pronounced the marriage of Catherine of Aragon and Henry VIII null and void. The king had been agitating for such a decision for the past six years and if that decision would not be made in Rome, then it was now possible in Canterbury. This was no ordinary decision by the archbishop, and the events which led up to it were no less than extraordinary. For in the process of seeking an annulment[1] of his first marriage, Henry VIII had done the unthinkable. The king of England, the 'Defender of the Faith', had led the Church in England out of obedience to the Church of Rome.

No one except Henry VIII ever really knew when he developed his famous scruples about his marriage to Catherine of Aragon for the first time. His confessor, Bishop Longland of Lincoln, remembered that Henry may have mentioned his misgivings as early as 1522 or 1523. If so, it was a well-kept secret until 1527, when the king informed first Cardinal Wolsey and then Catherine of his concern. Prior to that Henry had been, on the whole, a dutiful husband. At first the marriage appeared to have the qualities of a chivalric romance: in 1513, for instance, Henry had raced home in advance of his army to present his queen with the keys to Tournai and Thérouanne, trophies of the desultory campaign of that summer in northern France. Henry also involved Catherine in affairs of state publicly, and he listened to her advice privately. This is not to say that he was not a king of his times. We know that he had extramarital affairs but, as Professor Elton points out, they were, 'for a king, almost ludicrously few'.[2] Nevertheless, one illegitimate son, Henry Fitzroy (later created duke of Richmond), was recognised by the king, and another child was suspected of being a royal bastard – William Carey, son of Mary Carey, married sister of Anne Boleyn. Even so, despite whatever early worries Henry may have had about the validity of his marriage, he does not seem to have turned away from his wife entirely until at least 1525, by which time his infatuation with Anne Boleyn had grown into something far more threatening to the peace and stability of the realm than a typical court romance.

The origins of the first marriage

The marriage between Catherine of Aragon and Henry Tudor came about as a result of the diplomatic machinations of Henry VII. Seeking recognition of the legitimacy of his dynasty and a strong continental alliance, he had, in 1489, signed the treaty of Medina del Campo and committed England to war with France in support of Spain. Apart from any other benefits that England might have realised through this treaty, it was agreed that the alliance should be sealed by the union of the two royal houses by marriage. By 1496, the negotiations had concluded and Catherine, daughter of Ferdinand and Isabella of Spain, was to be married to the heir to the English throne, Arthur Tudor. After some delay, while the kings haggled over the bride's dowry and other financial considerations, Catherine arrived in England in October 1501 and was married in November. The marriage lasted just five months. Arthur, never as robust as his younger brother, died of consumption in April 1502, leaving the marriage alliance in tatters, Catherine a stranger in a strange land, and Henry VII with a diplomatic problem. After the death of his own queen in 1503, Henry VII briefly contemplated taking Catherine for himself but was persuaded against this. He chose to follow the first course of action which had suggested itself after Arthur's death: Catherine would be passed on to the next eligible Tudor heir, Prince Henry.

It was not that simple. Under normal circumstances such a marriage could not take place. In canon law (the laws of the Church) there were a number of reasons why a marriage might be deemed unlawful and therefore prohibited. Usually these impediments arose as a result of some existing relationship between the two parties proposing to be married. Close blood relationship, for instance, was regarded as an impediment, although the Church at the time considered even fourth cousins to be too closely related – a somewhat more extensive prohibition than exists today.[3] There were, however, other ways of establishing a relationship which might prove a hindrance to marriage, and Henry and Catherine were connected in at least two of these.

In the first place, they were related because Catherine and Arthur had been married – Henry and Catherine were 'in-laws', and any marriage between them would be considered scandalous by the Church. This was referred to in canon law as an offence against 'public honesty'. This relationship need not have been a serious obstacle, however, as the offence was a matter of human law and design, and there was no question of overturning any commandment or law of God. While it could not be ignored, it could be put in order easily. The Pope could grant, for good and sufficient reason, his special permission (a bull of dispensation) that the previous relationship be ignored and that a new marriage take place.

In the second place, Henry and Catherine were related to one another by what was known as 'affinity'. Affinity was a relationship which was thought to be established by sexual intercourse. In other words, if Catherine and Arthur had consummated their marriage, then Catherine and all of Arthur's relations were related in a way which could not be overlooked. Unlike an impediment on the grounds of an offence against public honesty, the prohibition of marriage between persons related by affinity was based not on human law or contract but on Scripture. Nevertheless, the established practice of the Church allowed the Pope to dispense with this impediment also if he found compelling reasons to do so.

All of this was known to Henry VII and his councillors when they came to consider making an application to the Pope to allow this new marriage. They, like everyone else, assumed that the first marriage had been consummated and appealed to Rome to remove the impediment of affinity. Pope Julius II granted this dispensation, and Henry Tudor was betrothed to Catherine of Aragon in 1503. All these points were to prove important later, as was the fact that the only dissenting voice in the whole of the process was that of Catherine herself, who, for reasons she never made public, always maintained that the dispensation had been issued in error: she claimed that her marriage to Arthur Tudor had never been consummated despite the fact that they had cohabited for some five months. Her complaint was ignored both in England and in Spain, and a dispensation for affinity was granted.

Apart from Catherine, everyone seemed to be pleased by the arrangement. An odd incident in 1505, when Prince Henry publicly disclaimed the marriage treaty and professed himself unwilling to honour it in any way, was the only sour note, but the reasons for this demonstration seem to have had little to do with his own wishes.[4] Indeed, virtually the first thing that Henry did when he came into his inheritance on the death of his father was to make his marriage official on 11 June 1509. If Henry had any doubts at all, they were forgotten in a headlong dash to wed the princess to whom he had been engaged for six years.

Scruples

Why, then, did Henry VIII become disenchanted with his wife? Human relationships are complex at the best of times, and Henry's reasons for wanting to rid himself of his wife after eighteen years of marriage are not simple. It is important to understand from the outset, however, that Henry was indeed sincere in his belief that he had been living in sin. Much of this sincerity may have to do with Henry's uncanny ability to convince himself of his own righteousness in most circumstances, but, once convinced, he was impossible to shift. That having been said, other reasons may have come into play.

By 1527, Catherine of Aragon was aged 42 and more or less past the age of childbearing; she was therefore vulnerable to Henry's discontent. Despite the fact that she had been pregnant often during their marriage, she and Henry had been singularly unsuccessful in producing a male heir who survived for very long. The fault was ascribed to her: Henry knew that he was

25

capable of producing healthy male offspring, as we have seen. But the king's only legitimate child who did manage to live past infancy was a girl, Mary, and she was not seen as a viable successor to the throne. England remembered all too well the chaos into which it could descend if the leadership at the centre was perceived to be weak: the reign of the ineffectual Henry VI and the Wars of the Roses which had consumed most of the latter half of the fifteenth century were not forgotten. There were no precedents in English history for women monarchs in any case, and those women who had attempted to win the crown or wield power (the Empress Matilda and, some would argue, Henry VI's wife, Margaret of Anjou) did not inspire confidence. Henry could not, of course, know that the sixteenth century would be notable for the number of strong women who managed the affairs of European states; nor could he know that one of his own daughters would govern with as much fame and success as any other monarch in the century (if not more). According to the wisdom of the times, a queen, as opposed to a king, was weak and might provide an opportunity for those who sought the restoration of a house far older than the house of Tudor. What is more, there were those still about who had better claims to the throne than the upstart Tudors or any of the bogus pretenders who troubled the first Tudor reign. The 'White Rose', Richard de la Pole, was alive until 1525 (he died at the battle of Pavia) and he had a powerful friend in the king of France. The Pole family, most of whom still lived in England and would eventually suffer at the hands of the Tudors, had Plantagenet blood, but there were others still who might be persuaded to remember distant claims that they might make on the crown if the Tudors appeared the slightest bit shaky. Henry was concerned for his dynasty and held it to be of no less importance than his father had before him. What came to be seen as Catherine's failure to produce the necessary ingredient for dynastic survival troubled him.

Catherine was also vulnerable because of the fluidity of European affairs. She was rapidly becoming a diplomatic liability to a king who was beginning to turn away from the old alliance with Spain which had been cultivated by Henry VII and which he himself had maintained in his early years. The traditional enemy, France, now began to look a likely ally after the new king of Spain and Holy Roman Emperor, Charles Habsburg, appeared to be in the ascendancy. Although a France ruled by the prematurely old and tired Louis XII had been Henry's early victim in 1513–14, a new French king, Francis I, had rudely awakened Henry from his dreams of past glory. Francis had shattered the Swiss in northern Italy at Marignano in 1515. The significance of this victory put Henry's much vaunted triumph at the battle of the Spurs in its proper perspective as a minor skirmish with no decisive outcome. In 1513, Henry had carried back the keys to two French towns; in 1515, Francis took all of northern Italy. While Francis held sway an English and Spanish alliance made a good deal of sense, but after the emperor crushed the French at Pavia in 1525 the situation altered.

Initially, Henry had seen Pavia as an opportunity to dispose of France once and for all. Despite his offer to renounce his claim to the French throne in a generous moment at the Field of Cloth of Gold some time earlier, Henry still dreamed of making that claim a reality. He wanted to join forces with the emperor so that they could carve up France between them. As the emperor was Catherine's nephew and had been friendly to England early on, Henry was confident of success. Charles Habsburg, however, had different ideas. He rejected both Henry's plans for France and the hand of Henry's daughter in marriage. This did not please the king of England. A realignment was taking place and there were those, notably the king's closest advisor, Cardinal Thomas Wolsey, who saw definite advantages in breaking the royal connection with the Habsburg family by annulment of the king's first marriage and seeking a more useful union elsewhere, even in France.

Catherine was made all the more vulnerable by the arrival at court of the young Anne Boleyn. Sister of a former mistress to the king, daughter of a prominent courtier and niece of the duke of Norfolk, Anne attracted much attention among the young men of the court. At length she caught the eye of the king but she did not follow her sister's path to the king's bed. Anne was made of entirely different stuff from Mary Carey and her vision was much more ambitious: she would not sleep with the king unless she was his lawful wife and queen. She was ambitious to be sure, but she was no fool and she was prepared to play a waiting game. She judged the king's temper and ego correctly: the more she refused him, the more he pursued her. The queen could not compete. Beautiful though she had once been, Catherine was the victim of time and too many pregnancies. What is more, she was always given to a strange and depressive type of religious devotion, and this tendency grew more pronounced as she grew older. Against this, Anne Boleyn must have seemed a breath of fresh spring air and all the more desirable for being bright, full of life and, as far as anyone knew, fit to bear children.

The situation, then, was not simple or straightforward. Henry had real concerns of a diplomatic and dynastic nature which served to make his marriage to Catherine of Aragon all the more unattractive by the mid-1520s. It would be wrong to assume that the king would be moved to contemplate the annulment of his first marriage simply because a young woman of the court refused to submit to him. Henry VIII was a man whose ego and appetites were as large as his daunting physical size, but he was not stupid. While the love that Henry professed for Anne Boleyn was important, it must not be thought that the king would have taken such drastic action had there not been other compelling reasons to cast off his eighteen-year marriage.

Whenever the idea first occurred to him and whatever weight he gave to his various reasons, by 1527 Henry VIII had resolved to end his marriage to Catherine of Aragon and take Anne Boleyn as his wife and queen. Henry had every reason to expect that the Pope would comply with his wishes, and there were recent precedents: the marriage of Anne of Brittany to the Emperor Maximilian I was a case in point and, closer to home, the duke of Suffolk had had his first marriage annulled. The process was straightforward enough: if Henry were to be granted an annulment he must seek it at the hands of the Pope and he must demonstrate some compelling reason why the marriage had been unlawful from its beginning. Henry was confident that he could show the original bull of dispensation to contain some fault which invalidated it. But in this he miscalculated. Popes were never eager to admit that they had made mistakes, nor were they happy to overturn decisions of their predecessors: in the earlier cases the circumstances had not required any reversal of a papal decision. Whatever case Henry chose to put would have to be a good one.

There were several approaches that might have been taken to prove the bull to have been in error. One approach was identified by Wolsey early in the process. Everyone was agreed that a dispensation of some kind was necessary for Henry to marry Catherine in the first place. The dispensation that had been issued appeared to be only for the impediment of affinity. If it could be proved that the bull had dispensed with a non-existent impediment (affinity) but had not dispensed with the actual impediment (public honesty), then the marriage would be seen to be invalid. Catherine, of course, had always maintained that her marriage to Arthur had never been consummated, despite what everyone else had assumed and the boasting of the adolescent Arthur on his wedding-night. She had always held that the dispensation should have been for public honesty, not affinity. Henry himself had on more than one occasion been heard to say that Catherine had come to him a virgin. It was a legal technicality and hardly a watertight case, as later canon lawyers were easily able to point out, but it could have served had circumstances been different.

A second approach, and one which Henry initially seized upon, was to question whether the Pope had the power to dispense the impediment of affinity at all. Henry knew that there were at least two passages in the Holy Scriptures which specific-ally prohibited the marriage of a man to his brother's widow.[5] The argument that Henry constructed on the basis of these two passages grew over the course of time. At first he seems to have allowed that the Pope might have the power to dispense the Levitical laws but had done so improperly in this case. As evidence he cited the problems that Catherine had in child-bearing. Because the prohibitions specifically stated that those who broke the law would be childless, Henry saw this as proof of the unlawful nature of his marriage. The fact that Mary had survived was irrelevant to Henry because, as king, he considered the production of a male heir all-important. Clearly, God was punishing him for breaking the Levitical laws by depriving him and the realm of a suitable heir to the throne.

As time went on, however, Henry's argument grew into an attack on the Pope's power to dispense any law that might be considered 'divine' rather than 'human'. The Levitical passages represented God's law and, as such, were beyond the com-petence of any Pope or human being to overrule or ignore. This attack on the Pope's authority made the writings of Tyndale and the early reformers very attractive to the king because they elevated the importance of the Word of God (the Holy Bible) above that of the traditions of the Church and the Pope. An enormous amount of time and energy was committed to proving this case, but with little success. The fact that there was a contradictory passage in the book of Deuteronomy which, far from prohibiting a man to marry his brother's childless widow, appeared to command it was a problem which was never really explained away satisfactorily.[6] What is more, the weight of the evidence from the early Christian Fathers, from more contemporary theological thought and from papal precedent was overwhelmingly against Henry's position. In fact, Henry's argument was never convincing to anyone who did not actively want to be convinced. The canon lawyers and theologians of Rome, and the supporters of Catherine of Aragon in England, had by far the better of the dispute.

A final approach was to challenge the assumptions under which the bull of dispensation was issued in the first place. Whenever a bull is granted to allow an action which would normally be contrary to canon law, some good cause must be shown for overlooking the canon law in question. This is true in all cases as dispensations are not simply issued arbitrarily. In the case of the dispensation which permitted Henry's marriage to Catherine, the cause that was cited in the bull was that the marriage would ensure peace between England and Spain. It was therefore argued that the bull was invalid because England and Spain were not at war, had been allies for some time before the marriage and needed no insurance of peace between them. The premise on which the bull was promulgated was false, in other words. Moreover, even if the premise were correct, was this a cause weighty enough to justify the human suspension of what was, after all, God's law? Technical problems with the bull were also seized on. The bull had been written as if Henry himself were making the request, but he was under age at the time and therefore incapable of suing for the dispensation. In addition, by the time the marriage was solemnised all those who had made the original application and for whom, presumably, the cause of peace had been so important were dead. This entire line of argument sought to challenge the motivation of Julius II in granting the original bull. As that motivation was seen to be faulty, the bull itself was therefore argued to be void.

At various times during the proceedings these arguments

surfaced and were pursued. In order to make his case, Henry turned to scholars, lawyers and theologians in England and, eventually, on the continent. Henry's quest for an annulment would become a drawn-out process, finally being thrown into the lap of the English Parliament. However, in the first instance, Henry turned to the most powerful man in England, apart from himself, to make his desires a reality: Thomas Cardinal Wolsey, archbishop of York, legate *a latere* (the Pope's personal representative) and chancellor of England.

Wolsey

Thomas Wolsey had risen from modest beginnings to a position of prime importance in the government of Henry VIII by a combination of hard work, good luck and inborn ability. Although, as one must be careful to remember, Henry VIII was always in charge despite the fact that he was never terribly interested in the day-to-day business of government (most especially in his early years), Wolsey, among all the king's councillors, came to dominate. Many who did not know the king assumed that Wolsey had a good deal more power than he did. Perhaps, in unguarded moments, even the cardinal himself believed this. Nevertheless, as Professor Guy has noted, although the king's ministers sometimes enjoyed a great degree of freedom in pursuing their policies and in managing the affairs of state, 'they operated within the limits of Henry's trust and confidence'.[7] This was true of all Henry's councillors, no matter how important they may have appeared: they did their jobs at the pleasure of the king, and those who displeased the king were in serious jeopardy – as both Wolsey and, later, Thomas Cromwell discovered.

Born in Ipswich in 1472, the son of a butcher, Wolsey possessed an intellect and ability which were recognised early. In a way that was more typical of previous centuries and was just beginning to change in the sixteenth, he made his way to power through the Church. After a series of ecclesiastical appointments which brought him to the attention of Henry VII, Wolsey's potential as a diplomat was recognised and he was entrusted with several missions of importance, gaining in consequence more substantial ecclesiastical offices for his support.[8]

31

After the death of Henry VII, Wolsey remained in government service and proved to be of invaluable assistance to the young Henry VIII during the French campaign of 1513. If this campaign was a success (and the king thought that it was despite the lack of any real strategic gains), Wolsey was in large part responsible for it and for the beneficial peace that was negotiated afterwards. Above all, it earned him Henry's trust. From about 1514 until his fall in 1529, Wolsey was Henry's most powerful minister.

In fact, Wolsey held unprecedented power for a subject of the Crown. By 1514 he had been made archbishop of York, and in the next year the Pope made him a cardinal. In 1515 he became chancellor of England. In 1524 he managed to have his status as a papal legate *a latere* made permanent (an unusual appointment) and so combined in himself enormous power over both the Church and the State: Wolsey was in a position to achieve much. His opportunities for the reform of the Church, of the government and of the legal system were limitless. All needed attention and in all areas he managed to make some changes. But he was criticised for his apparent lack of scruple and because he was known to be one of the worst offenders in those abuses for which the clergy were starting to be maligned. He was a notable pluralist, always holding more than one bishopric and a host of other Church offices besides; he ignored his promise of celibacy and was the father of several children; he appointed his own children to benefices and was guilty of both nepotism and the ordination of minors; and he was known to sell ecclesiastical offices (simony). All of his reforms, whether in the Church or in the government or the law, were tinged with the suspicion that they were undertaken with his own best interests at heart – and this was true to a large extent. His arrogance and his ostentatious display of his personal wealth were also resented and he made many enemies at the English court: this would prove critical later when Anne Boleyn and her supporters actively worked against the cardinal. Whatever his worth as councillor to the king and leader of the Church, Wolsey was viewed by many as exemplifying all that was wrong with the Church and all that was in need of changing.

However, Wolsey was most interested in foreign affairs. It was obvious that the most powerful monarchs in Europe were Francis I of France and Charles V, the Holy Roman Emperor.

The struggle between these two was central in European affairs, and Wolsey was determined to keep both England and himself as close to the centre as possible. The question was, where did England fit into the struggle between these two sixteenth-century super-powers?

As Wolsey attempted to answer this diplomatic question, Henry approached him in 1527 with the news that he was interested in seeking an annulment of his marriage with Catherine. Far from being closed to the idea, Wolsey saw some real possibilities. But the king had not made his intention to marry Anne Boleyn clear to his minister; if he had, Wolsey might have received Henry's news with less enthusiasm. To the chancellor, Catherine was a symbol of a previous alliance which had outlived its usefulness. Securing the annulment and the king's remarriage to a French princess might be a more advantageous arrangement for England. It never occurred to Wolsey that the king was making all this fuss over a pretty young girl at court, and he was horrified when the truth of the king's intentions finally became obvious. Yet Wolsey was prepared to do all that he could to further the king's desires – that had always been his worth to the king and it would remain so. As legate *a latere*, Wolsey had the power to make the necessary judgement in this case. He could grant the annulment in the name of the Pope but his decision would not be final: should Catherine choose to appeal against his decision, the case would automatically revert to Rome, where there was no certainty that it would be resolved in the king's favour. There was little doubt that Catherine would make such an appeal. This would, of course, complicate matters and, as we shall see, as time went on the likelihood of a decision at Rome in Catherine's favour became almost inevitable. Henry, on the other hand, wanted absolute certainty that his annulment would be granted, and so he and his chancellor moved swiftly and secretly.

In May 1527, Wolsey called the king before a secret tribunal. Wolsey sat with the archbishop of Canterbury, Warham, to establish whether the king's marriage was lawful. Acting in his capacity as legate *a latere*, Wolsey would hear the king's explanation for a marriage which appeared to be in violation of canon law. Once Henry had put his case, Wolsey would declare the marriage in violation of the law and therefore annulled. This would be confirmed by the Pope, and Henry would be free to marry whomever he wished. This plan was destroyed by two problems. First, once she got wind of what was being planned, Catherine was not prepared to cooperate and immediately began to make plans to appeal to Rome. Second, Charles V sacked Rome in May 1527 and the Pope became the prisoner of the emperor.

Catherine had no intention of allowing the case to be settled in England. She wrote immediately to her nephew, Charles V, and informed him of what her husband was up to. Henry, with staggering ineptitude, failed to prevent this news from reaching Charles even though he knew that the letter was written and who was to carry it. Once Charles understood what was happening he made his displeasure very clear to Henry. Even so, this did not necessarily mean that Henry's cause could not get a favourable hearing at Rome. After the sack of Rome, the Pope was in desperate need of friends and welcomed English interest in his plight. English support for the Pope might, therefore, be traded for the Pope's compliance in the 'King's Great Matter'. Plans were laid to allow Wolsey to set up a kind of papal court in exile at Avignon while the Pope was in captivity and there exercise near-papal powers by proxy while Pope Clement was unable to act. It was a good plan, but Wolsey was stymied; the plan relied on the cooperation of the College of Cardinals, which, for a variety of reasons, refused to go along with Wolsey's idea. The final blow was the release of Pope Clement VII in December 1527 which rendered the plan unviable. Failing in this, Wolsey and Henry attempted to get the Pope to grant the power to decide the case in England without the right of appeal.

By the end of 1527, the situation in Italy was fluid again. The French were back in strength and the Pope, although no longer resident in Rome, was not under the emperor's direct control. English ambassadors were sent to the Pope to urge him to grant Wolsey the power to decide the case without referral to Rome, but Clement was not disposed openly to support Henry's case. His position was tenuous. He knew the power of the emperor only too well and was afraid that French control in northern Italy was only temporary: he hedged his bets. In the summer of 1528, he sent Cardinal Campeggio to England with the necessary powers to resolve the annulment. However, these powers were to be kept secret and Campeggio was instructed to delay until the political situation in Italy became clearer. Campeggio found enough reasons to put off hearing Henry's case until May 1529, by which time it was apparent that the emperor was not going to allow the French to dominate Italy. In June the battle of Landriano decided the issue. The French were defeated and the Pope signed the treaty of Barcelona, swearing his support for the emperor and the empire. In England, Campeggio adjourned the hearing of Henry's case, ostensibly for the summer: in fact, it was apparent to all observers that the case would never be heard. Wolsey had failed, and there were those who were poised to take advantage of his failure. The supporters of Anne Boleyn now moved against Wolsey in strength.

The king was no closer to his annulment. He became increasingly frustrated by the cardinal's lack of success and began to look elsewhere for solutions. Suggestions were made as early as July 1529 which were designed to deal with the king's problems and, not incidentally, destroy the power of the cardinal. Lord Darcy submitted a variety of complaints against Wolsey, and proposed a Parliament to deal with both the cardinal and a number of perceived evils in the Church. Anne Boleyn's supporters had even begun to suggest that the entire matter ought to be dealt with in England and that the solution might be found in the destruction of papal authority in the realm.[9] Although not entirely persuaded, Henry was moved not only to dismiss Wolsey but to call a Parliament to meet in November 1529. In doing so Henry 'let slip the dogs of war' against Rome and took the first step down the road to Reformation.

3

The break with Rome

By the late summer of 1529, all the king's plans were in tatters. He had hoped, of course, to achieve his annulment with a minimum of fuss, but an uncooperative Catherine of Aragon and an ever-changing political situation in Europe had made a nonsense of such efforts. Henry could count on no help from Catherine herself; the idea that she would willingly go along with the divorce or that she would simply roll over without an appeal to Rome if presented with a *fait accompli* was always far-fetched.

Henry was furious. While Wolsey might be punished for his failures, this still left the king no closer to his goal. Realistically, there was little Henry could do. Few good ideas suggested themselves immediately, and those that were put forward were rather too radical for a king who, despite his injured pride, was not yet prepared to defy the Pope and the Church to the point of schism. In so far as there was a policy after the disastrous summer of 1529, it was to try to convince the Pope to bend to the king's will. However, the methods to achieve that policy were unclear. The government began to drift, and important factions struggled to dominate the court.

The most important of these factions was in the Privy Council. Led by the duke of Norfolk and including Lord Darcy and Stephen Gardiner (now bishop of Winchester), its members were religious conservatives and had all played an important part in the downfall of Cardinal Wolsey. Although they were intent on pleasing the king, they had few constructive contributions to make on the matter of the divorce. A second faction was made up of supporters of Anne Boleyn, who was herself a powerful and manipulative influence on the king. The members of this faction were prepared to suggest far more radical solutions to the king's problems. Including such men as Thomas Cranmer and Thomas Cromwell, they tended to be influenced by radical religious opinions and were therefore 'not afraid to extend royal power in Church and state at the clergy's expense'.[1] To these men, the simplest way to deal with the Gordian knot of the divorce was to cut it in two, to act independently, and if that meant a clean break with the Church of Rome (as it most assuredly did), then so be it. The third important faction at court was composed of those who supported the queen. Including such prelates as Bishops John Fisher and Cuthbert Tunstall, and the lawyer Thomas More, they were committed to the defence of the Church and Catherine. They could not be ignored. Fisher, in particular, proved an eloquent and tenacious opponent of the divorce as well as standing firmly against the inroads made by the Protestant heresy. Thomas More soon became valuable to the faction for reasons beyond his obvious intellectual skills.

The immediate result of such a faction-ridden court was to create a kind of paralysis of policy. Henry's appointment of More as chancellor in Wolsey's place had been intended to break the political stalemate: initially the king was unaware of More's support for Catherine. A brilliant common lawyer and a humanist who was concerned about the state of the Church but committed to it, More may have appeared acceptable to all parties and capable of bringing about some kind of consensus. But his appointment proved to be a mistake. His much-vaunted and valued integrity would not allow him to accept the post unless Henry was aware that he could not support the divorce. While this disappointed the king, More was still given the post as he was the best man available and on the understanding that he would not be asked to involve himself in the matter of the divorce. More's position as chancellor necessarily made him privy to the king's plan, an awkward position for one who supported the queen, but one which he may have used to her advantage.[2] The situation was uncertain. From the summer of 1529 until the ascendancy of Thomas Cromwell in 1532, Henry cast about for a clear way forward.

The Reformation Parliament

It might be attractive to see Henry's call for a Parliament as part of a cunning master-plan to deal with his domestic troubles without recourse to Rome and, in the process, to take to himself the power and wealth of the Church. This has, of course, been suggested and there were those about him who saw much to be gained were the king to use Parliament to break the power of the Church in England. However, there is little evidence to suggest that this was ever in Henry's mind when he issued the summons in August 1529.[3]

In fact, Henry's reasons for calling Parliament when he did are not immediately apparent. It may have been his original intention to use the Parliament as a platform to deal with Wolsey. Indeed, Lord Darcy's articles (see p. 35 above) amounted to a compilation of charges to be made against the cardinal in Parliament, effectively accusing him of treason. By the time Parliament actually sat, Wolsey had been dealt with by other means: Henry had not forgotten his good and faithful servant and moved to protect him from the mortal danger that a Parliament would have exposed him to. Wolsey might be disgraced but he would not be destroyed.

But Wolsey had made many enemies in his time and they were by no means finished with him. If Wolsey were not permanently removed from the scene, there was always the chance of a recovery. Those who had particular reasons for hating the former chancellor, such as Anne Boleyn, who blamed him for the failure of the divorce effort, might see a Parliament as a way of attacking the cardinal indirectly. There was sufficient animosity in all quarters to suggest that much of the action taken against the Church in the first session of the Reformation Parliament far from being designed to challenge papal jurisdiction in England, was aimed at preventing Wolsey from making any kind of political come-back.[4] Yet Henry does not appear to have had any intention of punishing his former chancellor any further by the time it met.

The sequence of events leading up to the Reformation Parliament may be helpful in understanding the king's decision to call Parliament. All through July 1529, it was increasingly apparent that the plans to resolve the divorce in England were doomed. On 23 July, Cardinal Campeggio adjourned the hearings for the summer on the thinnest of pretexts, and in the light of political events in Italy it seemed unlikely that anything further was to be gained by travelling down this route. Unable to secure his divorce in the relatively safe courts of England, and with Rome hostile to his intentions, Henry had very few options left open to him. On 9 August, Henry issued the necessary summonses for a Parliament. On the same day, he took steps to bring Wolsey before the court of King's Bench on charges of violating the Statutes of Provisors and Praemunire, in essence protecting Wolsey from Parliament. By September it was clear that the king had softened towards his former counsellor, despite the pressure he was coming under from Wolsey's enemies. He made a number of gestures which were conciliatory. He granted the cardinal an interview (over the strenuous objections of Anne Boleyn); he sent a gift; more importantly, he threw Wolsey a life-line. Although indicted at the King's Bench and stripped of his power and most of his wealth, Wolsey was not thrown into prison and was permitted to keep some of his property. It was not beyond the bounds of possibility that Wolsey might recover power, and the cardinal's enemies knew it. This point was hammered home soon after Parliament met in November, when Henry remitted part of Wolsey's sentence.

But if the king did not intend to summon a Parliament to destroy Wolsey, what other reason could he have had? Faced with the fact that he had run into a dead-end in trying to pursue his divorce down a more or less usual road, with a divided and faction-ridden court, and with an increasingly uncertain diplomatic scene, it may very well be that the king considered that summoning Parliament was the only constructive move that he could make. And so on 3 November, amid great pomp and ceremony, the Parliament convened at Blackfriars with only the vaguest of purposes. Thomas More's opening address did not make matters any clearer. The crimes alleged against his predecessor were enumerated but it was made clear that deciding the penalties for those crimes was out of the hands of the Parliament, as Henry wished it to be. The only reasons that More could summon up for the gathering of the Lords and Commons were that certain laws were in need of bringing up to date, and that new laws were needed to deal with problems that had only recently been discovered among the people. While there is no surviving copy of this speech, all reports of it are similar; what is striking is that it was no more specific than it was. Which were the laws that needed reworking? What new problems had arisen? It was all very vague. The Parliament met without any clear direction from the government and without any clear idea of what it was expected to do.

Once the Parliament met, however, there were those who were able to use it for their own ends. The Mercers' Company of London presented a list of grievances to do with trade but included one article which was extremely critical of the clergy. This anticlerical article found supporters in the Commons and, after a discussion in the House, a committee was assembled to draw up legislation to deal with the abuses that had been raised. Three bills emerged. They did not reflect the full extent of the abuses discussed – the debate in committee had been far-ranging – and the Commons may have been uncertain of just how far they could go, but they touched on several sensitive matters.

The first bill to be presented dealt with the practice of mortuary fees.* In practice there was no set fee, and the clergy usually demanded what they thought could be paid. Often fees were waived entirely, but some felt that the practice was offensive and had been abused. It was the refusal to pay the mortuary fee, for instance, that had been the flashpoint for the Hunne case (see p.16 above), and there were those in the House who would have remembered that case very well. The Commons passed the bill regulating mortuary fees without difficulty and there was little or no objection made in the Lords when the bill first came up for debate.

Probate fees* had been another bone of contention identified by the Commons. In drawing up the second bill, the Commons alleged that the Church courts charged excessive fees for probate, that the process was delayed unnecessarily in order to extract further fees and that bribery was common practice. Whereas there had been general agreement in the Lords that mortuary fees were in need of regulation, the bishops in the Lords did not concede the necessity to regulate probate fees. The bill had also been written in language that some of the bishops in the Lords found offensive. Their reaction was predictable: they were loudly opposed to the bill. The leading voice in opposition was that of John Fisher, bishop of Rochester, who openly accused the framers of this bill of a lack of faith and hinted at heresy. It was an intemperate outburst and led to an angry riposte from the Commons and an interview with the king, who was displeased. Despite the ill-feeling all around, committees with members from both Houses were set up to consider both the bills before them. When the Lords Spiritual would not be moved from their opposition, a long and acrimonious debate followed which saw the sympathies of the temporal Lords begin to swing towards the Commons.

The clergy were sufficiently well represented in the Lords to be able to prevent the bills from being enacted. In order to break the deadlock, Henry used a subtle threat. Probate and mortuary fees were not the only issues facing Parliament and so Henry used other legislation to demonstrate his displeasure with the clergy blocking the anticlerical bills. In exchange for the passage of a bill which relieved him of some £350,000 of debt incurred through forced loans, the king offered a general pardon. General pardons were nothing new and included the usual exceptions for capital offences, but this pardon, pointedly, did not extend to clergy guilty of violations of the Statutes of Praemunire or Provisors. Both of these statutes had served as willows with which to whip the clergy into line in the past, and excluding them from the general pardon suggested that the king might wish to use them again. The clergy took the point, and the bills regulating probate and mortuary fees were passed into law, albeit in a somewhat revised form.

If the clergy had taken the hint with regards to mortuary and probate fees, they still offered stiff resistance to the third bill aimed at clerical reform, that emerged from the Commons during this session. This bill was intended to limit the practice of pluralism and non-residence, as well as restricting the kinds of businesses – usually agricultural – the clergy might hold in addition to their cures. The justification of pluralism and non-residence had always been that it provided necessary income for clergy whose talents could be used best outside the parochial ministry as chaplains to bishops or nobility, as diplomats or as civil servants. While there had been abuses (Thomas Wolsey was always pointed to as the arch-abuser), the practice, if regulated, was seen as necessary. The Church felt that the regulations imposed on pluralism and non-residence were already adequate and it was here that the bishops in the Lords drew the line at lay interference in the governance of the Church. The king was again prevailed upon to find a solution and he did so with another joint committee. The lay members of the committee were not persuaded by the arguments put forward by the bishops, and positions hardened. Pressure was brought to bear and a compromise was reached. The bill that emerged was diluted with innumerable exceptions and qualifications in order to make it acceptable to the bishops, but one proviso remained particularly disturbing for some: applications for papal dispensations for non-residence were prohibited. In an uncertain and halting way the attack on papal jurisdiction had begun, even if most of those who passed this bill were unaware of its full import.

A precedent had been set. Now the Reformation of the Church no longer seemed to be a matter for the Church itself but one for the laity and, in particular, for Parliament. The Convocation of Canterbury, the ecclesiastical equivalent of Parliament which traditionally met at the same time, manifestly failed to enact any significant internal reforming legislation and by default, then, appeared to be surrendering the field to the laity. Those who supported Catherine of Aragon recognised the danger at once. As Professor Guy points out, 'if Parliament could reform the clergy, perhaps it could instruct the bishops to pronounce the divorce'.[5] Whether Parliament had overstepped its competence in passing the bills for the reform of the clergy became a moot point: Parliament clearly felt that it had the competence to legislate in such matters. When the Parliament broke up before Christmas it was apparent that the initiative now lay outside the Church. While this did not make the break with Rome inevitable, it did provide the king with another avenue to explore in pursuit of his divorce.

The assault on the clergy

Parliament had originally been prorogued until just after Easter 1530. As it was, it did not meet again until January 1531. The official reason given for the postponement was that there was plague in London, which there most assuredly was. However, there were other good reasons why Henry was content to leave the Parliament suspended for the time being.

All through 1530, the king was concentrating primarily on

42

resolving the divorce issue. Nevertheless, no sense of a coherent plan emerges and it may very well be that Henry had no clear idea of what to do. He was certainly not planning to break with Rome at this point. He solicited the favourable opinions of the major universities in Europe, but this would do little to persuade the Pope of the justice of his cause and, in any case, most of these opinions were hardly unequivocal in his favour. In March 1530, as part of the process set in motion by Catherine's appeal, the Pope ordered Henry to Rome so that the case might be settled. Although urged to take some kind of action, the king chose delaying tactics. In June he sent to the Pope a letter signed by eighty-three of the king's supporters, ingenuously wondering why his case had not been acted upon favourably and issuing the veiled threat of schism. The Pope was neither impressed nor worried by this, and his reply was patronising and calm. At Rome, Henry's ambassadors were appealing for a postponement in the proceedings at the very least. Hopes that the divorce could be settled without drastic measures being taken were receding even further.

However, in the late summer of 1530, Henry received a massive work put together by Thomas Cranmer and Edward Foxe entitled *Collectanea satis copiosa*. The document was a collection of historical and legal evidence from ancient sources which 'proved' that the divorce desired by Henry was justified and, more importantly, established that the king of England had always enjoyed sovereignty over the Church within his realm. Drawing heavily on the Holy Scriptures, some dubious historical traditions and the work of the fifteenth-century supporters of the Conciliarist movement (who argued for the supremacy of General Councils over the authority of the Pope), the evidence as presented suggested that Henry could act on his divorce unilaterally and that Rome had no right to interfere.

Even so, Henry was not ready yet to break with Rome. The opinions of the European universities and the *Collectanea* were seen as tools with which the Pope might be persuaded to grant the divorce, not as the theoretical foundation for schism. As there was little else Henry could do by the autumn of 1530 other than attempt to put some kind of pressure on the Pope, he did this by attacking the clergy with the powers he already had in law.

His first moves were hesitant. He identified fifteen clergy, most of whom were found among Catherine's supporters, and accused them of Praemunire in that they had accepted Wolsey's authority as a papal legate. The charge was based on a technicality – as we have seen, kings always felt at liberty to ignore this statute – but it was, nevertheless, intimidating. These cases were never pursued because, as early as October 1530, a new plan was devised which would charge all the clergy with Praemunire.

Originally, Henry may have been persuaded to expand on this theme by councillors fearful of a recovery of power by Wolsey. In 1530 the cardinal was stirring again and plotting against his enemies. This was taken as an ill omen by those who still feared him. A blanket charge of Praemunire against the clergy for accepting Wolsey's authority would clearly discredit the cardinal and cut away any support he might still command. The first move was to arrest Wolsey and neutralise him in the autumn of 1530. This policy proved all the more effective when the cardinal died late in November 1530, ending his bid to regain power for ever. But the idea of applying pressure on all the clergy still seemed a good way of pressurising the Pope even though Wolsey was gone. When Parliament reconvened on 16 January 1531, the Convocation of Canterbury was already in session and already worried about what the king might do.

What Henry intended became clear very early in the session. He offered the clergy a pardon for their crimes if they would pay an enormous sum of over £118,000 by way of a subsidy to protect the realm from either rebellion or invasion.[6] The clergy did not see the imminence of invasion quite as clearly as Henry claimed to see it but after some initial resistance, while the clergy still thought they had some room to manoeuvre, it became apparent that the king was in an uncompromising mood. When it was pointed out that under the Statute of Praemunire all clerical property could be forfeit to the Crown, the clergy agreed to Henry's demands. The financial exactions that Henry demanded were bad enough, but when it became apparent in the prologue to the articles (which were the instrument of the subsidy) that Henry was claiming more than the clergy's cash, the reaction in Convocation was furious. Henry was now demanding that the clergy recognise him as supreme head of the Church and clergy, a demand that the clergy could not agree to in the slightest. By some hard bargaining Archbishop Warham was able to find a compromise solution whereby

44

Henry might be entitled 'singular protector, only and supreme lord, and as far as the law of Christ allows even supreme head': as the law of Christ (by this the clergy understood canon law) would not allow Henry to be supreme head in the place of the Pope, this effectively negated his claim. But the political reality, that the king might effectively extort money and other concessions from the Church, left the clergy in a state of shock. The silence that greeted the announcement of this compromise in February 1531 was taken as assent, but it was hardly unambiguous. In effect the clergy were watching their independence being taken away and there was little they could do about it, despite the fact that they had managed to deflate the king's claims to supreme headship with a qualifying clause that made a nonsense of them. The damage was done. Parliament had already invaded areas that the Church was responsible for by legislating on ecclesiastical reforms. Now the king was claiming for himself the authority over the Church which had always belonged to the Pope. The pardon that Henry had promised to the clergy passed through Parliament just before the session closed at Easter, and some among both the clergy and the laity must have wondered just how far the king was willing to go to secure his divorce.

Despite the pressure Henry was bringing to bear on the clergy in his own realm, he made little headway at Rome. The Pope had forbidden Henry to remarry, and if he had not specifically ruled on the validity of the first marriage as he was being encouraged to do by Charles V, this was hardly seen as a hopeful sign. Henry's patience was wearing thin. The third session of Parliament met in January 1532 and would prove to be critical. Whereas in 1531 he had made demands with menaces and seen modest results, in 1532 he would take firm action. In this he was assisted by Thomas Cromwell.

Cromwell

Thomas Cromwell was born sometime around 1485 and had a chequered career. A mercenary, a merchant and, finally, a common lawyer, he was a man of both experience and great gifts. In many ways he was a chameleon – sympathetic to Protestantism and the anticlerical temper of the times, he nevertheless served Wolsey faithfully as an attorney and rose to importance in the cardinal's service. When Wolsey fell, Cromwell did not desert him but continued to manage the cardinal's business and to communicate with him, even though, as a Member of Parliament in 1529, Cromwell was actively working against the clergy by taking a leading role in the framing of anticlerical legislation.

In the vacuum created by the fall of Wolsey, Cromwell's organisational and administrative gifts stood out. He was a man of intelligence and vision and if he was later criticised for ruthlessness, he was without rancour or vindictiveness. Cromwell was purposeful and directed. It has been argued that he was the architect of a 'revolution' in Tudor government in that he took what was essentially the medieval household system and transformed it into a modern bureaucratic state.[7] He has also been credited with putting the concept of an 'Imperial kingship' into practice, whereby the king commanded not only temporal but spiritual affairs in his realm in much the same way as the first Christian emperor, Constantine, was thought to have done. While this analysis has been challenged since it was first put forward, there can be little doubt that Cromwell was responsible for significant changes made in Tudor government. What is more, if these ideas did not originate with Cromwell and were very much a collaborative effort on the part of theologians, lawyers and political theorists of the day as well as the king, Cromwell was nonetheless pivotal in the development of legislation which established the theory and practice of Tudor government throughout the rest of the sixteenth century.[8] In 1532, Cromwell brought forward a solution to the king's problems. Having proved useful to the king, he now became the 'principal manager of parliamentary affairs'.[9]

Cromwell had been at the centre of the anticlerical debates of 1529 and, although only three reform bills had been introduced, the discussion of clerical abuses had been wide-ranging. Cromwell had been deeply involved in the framing of two petitions in 1529 which were never presented to the king. Both were highly critical of Church policy but the second made the point that the ordinances passed by the Convocations were outside the authority of the king. This petition was revived by Cromwell in 1532 as the 'Supplication against the Ordinaries',* and presented to the king in March. Henry passed this document on to the Convocation of Canterbury. For centuries the Church had existed as a kind of state within the state. Responsible for making its own laws and enforcing them, it had preserved a useful, if largely theoretical, independence. Now a new message was being sent: the government was threatening to invade the traditional prerogatives of the Church and deprive the clergy of their right to govern themselves. Despite a spirited defence, drawn up principally by Stephen Gardiner, the king was not moved and publicly declared that he was displeased that the clergy appeared to be divided in their loyalties between king and Pope.

While the king was pursuing this train of thought, he made the first direct attack on the Church of Rome with the First Act of Annates. Annates were a payment that all bishops made to Rome before they were confirmed in their sees, and they represented a significant portion of a bishop's yearly income. They also represented one of the more important sources of papal revenue from England. Objected to by Wyclif in the late fourteenth century, they were a long-standing grievance as most bishops were forced to borrow heavily to meet the cost. Henry now moved to end the payment of annates on the grounds that they represented too heavy a burden on the bishops and that they took too much money out of the realm. In anticipation of the Pope's response to this, which would have been to withhold his permission to create new bishops in England, the bill provided for the consecration of bishops without papal authority. This radical move, which amounted to ignoring papal authority, was not easily passed in Parliament. The bishops in the Lords, even though the bill would relieve them of the obligation to pay annates, were opposed because of its assault on papal jurisdiction and, possibly, saw opposition as a way of registering their disapproval of the 'Supplication'. Many of the lay members of Parliament were also unsure, forcing the king to take the unusual (perhaps innovative) step of calling for a division in the House.[10] The stiff opposition to the bill forced Henry to include a clause which made the bill subject to confirmation by the king by letters patent. Although not part of his original plan, the clause was useful not only in allowing the passage of the bill but in adding another dimension to it. Having succeeded in bullying the clergy earlier, now Henry could try the same tactic with the Pope: if the Pope acceded to Henry's wishes in the matter of the divorce, the bill would be forgotten; if not, the bill would be enforced.

When this bill had passed through Parliament, Henry turned his attention to the Convocation of Canterbury and to the earlier theme of the independence of the clergy within his realm. In May 1532, Henry sent the clergy meeting in Convocation a list of demands which clearly restricted their rights to legislate for the Church independently of royal authority. The articles he submitted to the clergy required that a royal licence be granted before any canons or ordinances were enacted by Convocation; that Convocation itself should not meet without the express permission of the king; and that a review of canon law should to be undertaken by a committee (half lay, half clerical) appointed by the king. Having already established the competence of Parliament to legislate for the reform of the Church, Henry summoned a deputation from the Commons and asked them to consider what ought to be done about the ambiguous position of the clergy. This was a clear threat designed to intimidate the clergy into taking action on the articles Henry had submitted to them. It worked. On 15 May, the formal submission of the clergy was approved by the Convocation, although it is evident that this represented more of a surrender than of actual approval. While the submission of the clergy had a devastating effect on them, it had one other important consequence: Thomas More resigned the chancellorship. With More gone, the radical faction under Thomas Cromwell now held the king's confidence.

Despite all this, Henry was still no closer to his divorce. By the end of 1532, however, the diplomatic situation had improved to the extent that Henry believed that he could see the light at the end of the tunnel. Any peace treaty between the two major continental powers, France and the Holy Roman Empire, was always going to be fragile, and the most recent treaty, agreed at Cambrai in 1529, proved to be so as well. While there were no immediate hostilities, Francis I was seeking some diplomatic advantage and gained it by announcing the betrothal of his son Henry Valois to Catherine de Medici, one of the Pope's relatives. Henry VIII revived the French alliance in the hope that with the support of Francis I, who now had some influence with the Pope, the divorce might be settled. It was not to be, but the possibility that Henry might finally achieve his annulment must have seemed real. Anne Boleyn, who had refused adamantly to share the king's bed before she was queen, was now apparently so confident of success that she finally relented, and she was pregnant before the end of 1532. This, of course, put things in a new light. Anne, who was able to manipulate the situation effectively, used her pregnancy to pressurise the king into taking some kind of firm action. One major block to progress had always been the refusal of Archbishop Warham to defy the Pope. In August 1532, however, Warham died and Henry was free to appoint anyone he chose to fill the highest of ecclesiastical offices in England. He selected Thomas Cranmer. A little-known scholar without ambition, Cranmer had been part of the Cambridge group that gathered in the White Horse Tavern. He had first come to Henry's notice when he helped to put together the *Collectanea*, and the gathering of opinions from the European universities had been his idea. He was certainly not a strong candidate for the position of archbishop but he was known to be a supporter of the faction of Anne Boleyn and Thomas Cromwell. His appointment, no doubt, owed much to their suggestion. Cranmer was willing to do what the king wished in a way that Warham never had been. Now, with an archbishop who would not thwart him, and convinced that Anne was bearing him the son and heir he desired, Henry married her on 24 January 1533.

The royal supremacy

For the time being, however, the marriage remained secret. Although Henry had finally taken the step that he had desired, the legal machinery had not yet been set up to give this marriage even the appearance of legality. The Pope had not annulled the king's first marriage and had expressly forbidden Henry to marry again. The answer to this problem was already being prepared. Using the evidence provided by the *Collectanea* and his own ideas, Cromwell devised the statute which would free the king from the Pope's jurisdiction. The Act in Restraint of Appeals became law in April 1533 and radically changed the relationship between the king and the Church in England. It did so by making claims about the nature of kingship in England which had not been articulated previously. The Act in Restraint of Appeals, in simplest terms, ended the practice of removing cases from English courts to Rome on appeal. The act claimed that all legal issues, whether ecclesiastical or secular, were to be settled in English courts deriving their authority only from the king. Catherine of Aragon, therefore, could not legally take her case to Rome. While this may appear to be only a simple extension or readaption of the Statutes of Praemunire and Provisors already on the books, the true importance of the act was to be found not in the articles which forbade appeals but, rather, in the theory of royal supremacy that Cromwell, its composer, outlined in the preamble.

The preamble to the Act in Restraint of Appeals made a number of claims about the nature of the kingship in England which, if not entirely new, were argued with a new and different emphasis. The claim that the Crown was imperial was not new, but Cromwell's emphasis on England as 'an empire' was. An empire was different from a kingdom in that it stood as a sovereign state and neither required nor allowed any interference from the outside. No matters, spiritual or temporal, were outside the competence of the state or its courts, and these had their authority from the king, who in turn had his authority from God. The Pope, then, was an irrelevance: his jurisdiction was unnecessary, his interference unwelcome. The preamble to the bill was much more radical than the articles themselves, which were really rather restrained.

While the bill was debated in Parliament, the Convocation of Canterbury met to consider the validity of the king's marriage. Having been granted the power to make a decision on the matter, and with Warham dead, the bishops were not slow to render an opinion favourable to the king. With the agreement of his Convocation, Cranmer had no trouble in making the necessary declarations to annul the king's first marriage and regularise the second. In July 1533, the Pope took the only action left open to him and threatened to excommunicate Henry. For his part, Henry issued the necessary letters patent to make the Act of Annates effective and withdrew his ambassadors at Rome. He also called for a General Council of the Church to settle the dispute between himself and the Pope, but this outcome was not seen as a serious possibility by any involved. In September, when it became apparent that Henry would not be shifted, the Pope excommunicated the king of England. At last, the issue of the divorce was settled, and in the process the most significant ties with Rome had been severed.

There was, of course, still much to be done after the Act in Restraint of Appeals to complete the break with Rome. Parliament had to turn its hand to dealing with the ramifications of royal supremacy. A second Act of Annates refined the first and set up systems for the election of bishops and abbots. Peter's Pence, a papal tax unique to England from the time of the Anglo-Saxon kings, was outlawed. The submission which had been extorted from the clergy in 1532 was now made official in statute, with the major alteration that ecclesiastical cases would now find their final appeal in chancery rather than in the archiepiscopal courts. Next, all licences and dispensations formerly sought from Rome would henceforth be acquired in England. Another statute made the clergy liable to pay to the king first-fruits (one year's income upon assuming a position) and tenths (an annual 10 per cent tax on income). The Succession Act of 1534 officially recognised that the marriage to Catherine was void and that the marriage to Anne was valid. It also made it treason to utter slander against the king's new marriage and, most importantly, called for an oath to be administered throughout the realm declaring the legality of Henry's marriage to Anne. Finally, late in 1534, the Act of Supremacy served as a kind of omnibus statute which put all Henry's claims, and particularly his claim to be 'Supreme Head of the Church of England', on the record in one place.

The break with Rome was now complete. Although initially this break did not involve a radical transformation of the theology of the Church, the jurisdictional issues had been settled. Those powers which had once been seen as belonging exclusively to the Pope now rested in the king. But the transition was not as easy as it might appear: there were important opponents to the course Henry had chosen, and as Henry and Cromwell moved forward through the 1530s some of this opposition became very dangerous indeed.

4

The progress of the Reformation

In 1525 a 16-year-old woman from Kent named Elizabeth Barton fell victim to some kind of hysterical illness. In the midst of one dramatic seizure she had a vision of the Virgin Mary who promised to heal the young woman. When a crowd witnessed the miraculous cure, a star was born. Many were convinced that Barton was a genuine mystic, but when she began to receive and pass on messages from the Virgin Mary which were critical of the king's determination to secure an annulment, she became more than a curiosity. Her celebrity gained her access to the powerful. On one occasion she even spoke directly to the king claiming that he would be dead inside a month if he were to divorce Catherine and marry Anne.

After he had broken with Rome and proclaimed Anne to be the queen, it was vitally important to Henry that Anne's queenship be accepted. The new queen was never very popular, and Barton and those who surrounded her were stirring up public sentiment against Anne. It was his recognition of this which led Henry to crack down on Elizabeth Barton and make an example of her. In September 1533, Henry had the so-called 'Nun of Kent' and a handful of her supporters arrested. Under interrogation Elizabeth admitted that she was a fraud and then made this confession at Paul's Cross where she was publicly humiliated. She and four others were burned in April 1534.

Whether Elizabeth Barton was a prophetess or a misguided

52

and pathetic innocent used by men with a political axe to grind is really beside the point. The Nun of Kent exposed a number of problems that faced Henry after the break with Rome. She had become a focus for those who opposed the king. Warham protected her while he lived. John Fisher seems to have believed that she was what she claimed to be. However, both Thomas More and Catherine of Aragon recognised the danger in becoming involved with the Nun of Kent and stayed well clear. Stories (mostly spurious) were spread by her supporters about her miracles, and her prophecies were used as direct evidence of God's displeasure with the king and his new queen. This kind of talk could be dangerous and it is not surprising that when the Treason Act was passed in 1534 it included clauses which made it an offence to speak against the king's second marriage or to call either the king or the queen a schismatic, a heretic or any other slanderous name.

Henry saw the danger of the opposition and acted to discredit and destroy its focal point. He would have gone further if he had been able. Not satisfied with the execution of Barton and the ring-leaders, he accused Fisher, and tried to accuse More, of complicity. Fisher was found guilty and forced to pay £300 to buy his way out of a life-sentence. More was left out of the final bill of attainder for the simple reason that he had never been deceived: although Henry was all for proceeding against his former chancellor, the Council found no evidence against More and persuaded the king to wait until a more opportune moment.

The opposition

From the first, there had been those who opposed the king's plans for a divorce and supported Catherine of Aragon. As the king's campaign was stepped up after 1529, their resistance also mounted. Throughout 1532 and 1533, for instance, a preaching mission in the north sought to defend the Church from the dangers of heresy that the king appeared to be bringing into his realm. In Bristol there was virtual war in the pulpits as opposition found its voice against the reforming ideas of Hugh Latimer. Much of the resistance came from monks, especially from the heads of some of the stricter orders such as the Observant

Franciscans and the Carthusians, and was to have dire consequences for the religious houses later.

But opposition was not only to be found among the clergy. As we have seen, some of the nobility were not entirely comfortable with the way the government was proceeding. Some went so far as to open lines of communication with the imperial ambassador to assure him that there would be adequate support in England were the emperor to decide to invade in support of his aunt. A few sabres were quietly rattled, but the idea of a rebellion at this time was a nonsense, and Charles V was not fooled by the talk of a few of the English nobility and their exaggerated notions of how much support they could command. This is not to say that the fact that there were those who were willing to enter into treasonous conversations with the imperial ambassador is not significant. It is indicative of misgivings about the king's policies, but those misgivings were never sufficiently serious among enough of the nobility to lead to general rebellion.

In addition, there was reluctance on the part of some of the lay members of Parliament to stand against the Pope: some, no doubt, were motivated by principle, others were worried that the Pope's retaliation might not be restricted to the excommunication of the monarch but would also include economic sanctions against the English cloth trade, which, after all, relied heavily on its markets within the Empire. This opposition was especially evident in the Commons debate on the Bill in Restraint of Appeals. Parliamentary opposition, however, could be and was dealt with effectively by political means – reason, persuasion and, if those failed, intimidation.

There was little the government could do directly to stop those who opposed the divorce from talking until the Treason Act came into effect. However, there were indirect means that might be used to muzzle the opposition. The Act of Succession of 1534 had required that all adult males in the realm swear an oath to the effect that the second marriage of the king was his only lawful marriage and that the succession should pass to any offspring of that union. Very few refused to comply when the oath began to be administered in the spring of 1534, even though the oath itself implied a denial of papal jurisdiction and authority. The inmates of most religious houses who had been so opposed to the king's policies were persuaded to swear acceptance, but a few resisted. The Carthusian monks of the Charterhouse in London refused and six of their number were seriously mistreated and eventually put to death. Several other clerics also perished for refusal to take the oath. However, by far the most notable of those who refused and suffered were Thomas More and John Fisher. Both were summoned to London to take the oath in April 1534. Both found themselves confined to the Tower soon thereafter.

Initially, Henry probably intended to try to intimidate both More and Fisher into swearing the oath. Both were men of eminence and both were known and respected widely through-out Europe – it would not do to treat them as roughly as he had the Carthusian monks. Henry hoped that a stay in the Tower might shake their resolve or, failing that, might at least isolate them from others who resisted and deprive the opposition of two of its most important leaders. The problem was that this strategy did not work. Henry had not reckoned on the strength of the principles of these two men. More and Fisher were not intimidated by the Tower, and those who continued to resist drew strength from their example. This proved extremely irrit-ating and when in May 1535 the Pope made the entirely empty gesture of elevating Fisher to the office of cardinal, Henry flew into a blind rage.

As must be clear by now, Henry VIII was a man of intelligence and great passions. Sometimes his passion held sway over his intelligence, and so it did in the spring of 1535. Although he had tried to avoid making his enemies martyrs and had been advised to caution by Cromwell and Cranmer, the Pope's futile action seemed an insult, and the intransigence of More and Fisher was insufferable. Cromwell did make a real effort to save More, whom he admired (he was less interested in Fisher), but the king was determined to destroy both men.

It was not hard to find evidence against Fisher. He had never made a secret of his opinions in the matter of the divorce and had fiercely defended the Church when Henry began his assault on its liberties. John Fisher was particularly eloquent and effective in the House of Lords, where he was the principal spokesman against the king's policies. He had strenu-ously objected to the three anticlerical bills of 1529 and continued to obstruct the government's plans whenever he could. But the bishop of Rochester's dedication to the cause of

Catherine of Aragon had led him to go too far. Although the government did not know it at the time, Fisher had been in correspondence with the emperor for some time, urging invasion. But this evidence was not necessary to convict him of treason, for his opinions on the royal supremacy, the divorce and the succession were well known and admitted to freely. In June 1535, he died on the scaffold, a martyr to his cause and his Church.

The case of Thomas More was entirely different. More was a common lawyer and a very good one at that. He had known since his resignation as chancellor that he was in jeopardy and had thought to retire quietly into private life, where he could keep his opinions to himself and save his conscience. The basis of his defence against the charges brought against him in the summer of 1535 was his silence when asked to take the oath (the legal interpretation of silence was acceptance, a principle invoked by Warham when he was greeted by the stony silence of Convocation after presenting the king's terms for the clerical pardon of 1531). He had steadfastly refused to discuss the issues surrounding the royal supremacy and the divorce. He had avoided becoming entangled with Elizabeth Barton and her supporters. But his scrupulous silence when called upon to take the oath did not save him. In the end the testimony of Sir Richard Rich, often supposed to be false, sealed More's fate. Rich claimed that More had spoken treason in his hearing, and this was enough to allow the judges to convict. Only after his conviction did More openly speak on the supremacy and reveal that his opinions were pretty much what everyone suspected them to be. More was executed in July.

The executions of More and Fisher effectively ended the opposition. While Henry VIII and Cromwell have been condemned, rightly, for the way in which they ruthlessly destroyed their enemies, their methods did achieve the ends intended. More and Fisher were martyrs to their cause; subsequently they were canonised. But they were dead and, for the time being, no longer any trouble. Europe was shocked but no action was taken. While there was general regret at their deaths, even among those who could not support their stand, no rebellion was sparked off and the opposition evaporated for the moment.

The dissolution of the monasteries and the Pilgrimage of Grace

It is difficult to know just how much land belonged to the Church in the sixteenth century. Estimates put it somewhere between one-fifth and one-third of all the land in England. It was from this land, granted to the Church over a long period of time, that the Church derived its income – bishops' stipends depended on episcopal lands, a vicar's income was determined by the lands with which his parish was endowed, and a monastery's lands provided the income for the maintenance of the house. The Church was generously provided for and the land that it held had been coveted by the laity for quite some time. The resumption of Church lands was not a new idea in the 1530s and had been in circulation since the fourteenth century. However, the Church as a whole was vulnerable now and, in particular, the monasteries were at risk.

There are several reasons for the increased vulnerability of the Church at this moment. We have seen that Henry had already assaulted the independent jurisdiction of the Church, and that the success of that attack weakened the Church. When threatening the clergy with a blanket accusation of Praemunire, Henry had made much of the split loyalties of the clergy, and this was especially true of the monastic orders, most of which were directly answerable only to the Pope. The monasteries were in a very ambiguous position after the momentous legislation of 1533–4. This ambiguity only served to strengthen the arguments which were being put forward by reforming preachers and writers, who were highly critical of the state of England's monastic houses and the perceived drift away from their founding principles. What is more, it was in the monastic orders that most of the resistance was found when the government was forcing acceptance of royal supremacy.

More to the point, the government was in a difficult financial position. Revenues had not been keeping pace with expenditure – unlike his father, Henry VIII was not reluctant to spend money, and his warlike impulses earlier in his reign had been expensive. Added to this, the threat of an invasion from the continent in support of Catherine of Aragon had induced the government to embark on a major project to shore up England's defences which was also a significant drain on resources.

57

Demands for parliamentary taxation were out of the question as long as the government needed Parliament to support it in its effort to end papal jurisdiction in England and secure the divorce. But traditional Crown customs revenues had fallen off because of changes in trade patterns, and the feudal prerogative of the king, so brilliantly exploited by Henry VII, was not producing the kind of income the Crown needed. Indeed, the Crown's increased claims to feudal revenue only engendered resentment, as evidenced in the difficult passage of the Statute of Uses in 1536 (which finally closed the legal loopholes which allowed evasion of feudal taxes due to the king). Cromwell even tried a revolutionary peacetime tax, but he saw clearly that the most fertile source of new revenue for the Crown would be the newly 'liberated' Church of England.

He began his efforts to increase Crown revenue at the expense of the Church by securing the payment of first-fruits and tenths to the government by statute in 1534. If the bishops thought that the Act of Annates (revised by a second Act of Annates in 1534) relieved them of the crushing burden of these payments, they were wrong. What the Pope would not be allowed to have, the Crown would now take. While the cash raised through this tax and other clerical taxes was important, amounting to some £400,000 over the next five years,[1] the real money was to be made by the assumption of Church property. Land, if managed properly, had the advantage of providing a regular income in the long term. It was clearly Cromwell's plan to put the Crown on a firm financial footing by transferring the wealth of the Church to the government.

In addition to the financial benefits, political advantage could be gained from taking Church lands. Cromwell was aware that the laity had always coveted the Church lands and he was also aware that there were many among the nobility and the gentry who were decidedly lukewarm in their support for royal supremacy. The sale of Church lands to the laity might be an inducement to them to become enthusiastic supporters of the government's policies, because, in order to protect their new landed interests, they would be less inclined to support threats to the new order which the government had instituted and which had benefited them in real terms.

To achieve this goal, the government needed to know what it had to work with. In January of 1535, Cromwell was appointed vicar-general of the Church and moved immediately to discover the worth of all Church property in England. In only six months his investigators put together the *Valor ecclesiasticus*, which was a comprehensive valuation of all that the Church owned. He now knew exactly what he had to gain and proceeded to launch his attack on monastic property. Commissioners were sent out to conduct a visitation of the monasteries in order to discover problems and, supposedly, rectify them. However, the exercise was cynical in its conception: Cromwell had no intention of solving problems but was intent on finding (or inventing) evidence which would prove that the monasteries were sufficiently corrupt to merit dissolution. Scandals were discovered. The evidence collected by Cromwell's commissioners was sufficient to allow the introduction of a bill into Parliament in 1536 which called for the dissolution of all monasteries in England with an income of £200 or less. As one historian has noted, it is remarkable how that level of income should have been so firm a dividing-line between virtue and depravity.[2] About 300 houses were involved. The actual process of dissolution was not complicated. Cromwell's commissioners visited the doomed houses, dissolved them formally, made an inventory of any movable wealth they possessed, and made provisions for the monks themselves. Some houses were permitted to buy their way out of the dissolution, but their reprieve was only temporary. By and large, the government dealt with the situation fairly. Monks were either moved to larger houses where they could continue in their vocation if they wished, moved to a parish ministry of some kind if they were qualified, or pensioned off. All outstanding debts that the house may have had were paid.

The dissolution of the monasteries met with a mixed reaction. In some areas, the houses gave up quietly and without any public outcry. In other places, particularly in the north, where monasticism retained some of its earlier strength and popularity, the commissioners met with stiff resistance. Here the immediate result of dissolving the monasteries was to bring the hitherto simmering opposition to the king's policies and the changes he had imposed to a hard boil which, for a time, appeared to threaten the Crown itself.

However, the trouble began not in the north but in Lincolnshire. Whipped up by rumour and anti-government preaching,

riots broke out in Louth in October 1536 and spread throughout the shire. In fact, this was not the beginning of a concerted
rebellion against the Crown and its policies; there were actually
three separate risings. The Lincolnshire rebellion lasted from 1
October until 18 October 1536; the rising in Yorkshire, known
as the Pilgrimage of Grace, lasted from October to December
1536; and a further set of risings in the north-west took place
sporadically in January and February 1537. Of the three the
Pilgrimage was the most dangerous.

The revolts had much common ground. The issues at stake
were complicated. Bad harvests, objections to the peacetime tax
imposed by Cromwell, and dislike of the Statute of Uses and of
Henry's revival of his feudal prerogatives all played a part.
While all these were included in the complaints of the rebels,
religious issues dominated the minds of those who rose. In
Yorkshire, the rebels chose to think of themselves as Pilgrims
and marched under the banner of the Five Wounds of Christ.
The north was conservative and distrusted the innovations that
it saw creeping into its religion. The dissolution of the smaller
monasteries was the final blow.

The Lincolnshire rebellion ended as quickly as it had started.
Having outlined their demands, which included not only their
objections to taxation, the Statute of Uses, innovations in
religion and the dissolution of the monasteries but also demands
for the dismissal of Cromwell, Cranmer and other reforming
bishops, the rebels waited for the king to respond. When it
became apparent that the king would not negotiate with rebels,
the resolve of the gentry leadership crumbled. They were not
inclined to risk all and persuaded the rank and file to disband.

A far more serious revolt began in Yorkshire only days after
Lincolnshire's abortive rebellion had begun. Under the leadership of the lawyer Robert Aske, some 30,000 men moved on
York. Their demands were virtually identical to those of the
men of Lincolnshire. The difference was that there was a great
deal more support for this rising among the nobility, including
Lord Darcy, the old foe of Wolsey, who was nevertheless not a
supporter of the royal supremacy. A rising of this nature was
dangerous indeed. Henry had only a small army under the duke
of Norfolk at his disposal and could not hope to defeat the
rebels in the field at this time. Had the rebels wished to press
home their advantage, a defeat of the duke would have left the

way clear to London. However, the rebels felt that negotiation was the best way to secure their demands and entered into an ill-fated discussion with Norfolk, who never had any intention of keeping the terms that he agreed to at the time. The Crown was buying time. Aske was in a very strong position at York, where he had taken over the government of the north, and may have felt confident that he could negotiate in good faith with the king's representative. The rebels' council met to finalise the Pilgrims' demands in early December, and when Norfolk offered a free pardon and appeared to agree to some of the rebels' demands Aske disbanded his army, sure of success.

When in January 1537 further disturbances took place in the north, the king and Norfolk moved swiftly. The new risings were used as an excuse for reneging on all that had been promised to Aske. Norfolk, now in a much stronger military position, moved to crush any signs of rebellion with brutal efficiency. Aske was arrested, as was Darcy, and both were executed. The north was impressed by the ruthlessness that the king had displayed and did not rise in force again during Henry's reign.

The defeat of the northern rebels left the way open for the continuation of Cromwell's policy for the dissolution of the monasteries. The larger monasteries had been exempted from the 1536 Act, but now the government moved to persuade them to dissolve themselves and turn their land over to the Crown. By 1540 the process was complete; monasticism was ended in England, and the Crown was enriched in the process. Much of the land that the Crown received from the monasteries was subsequently sold off. By far the bulk of this was bought by the gentry, whose importance in English society grew as a result. In all, the Crown would see a profit of about £1.3 million in proceeds from sales of lands, from goods and from rents.[3] An entirely new financial office, the Court of Augmentations, was set up by Cromwell to deal with the money which now came to the Crown as a result of the dissolution. Important though the dissolution of the monasteries was to the government financially, it was also indicative of the changes taking place in religion in England. Most of the monasteries were reduced to ruins quickly. Of course, any valuables that the monasteries possessed found new homes with the wealthy. Lead, a valuable commodity, was taken from the roofs and sold. Builders removed the stones from the walls for other constructions. Glass was removed from windows. Some old monastic houses were preserved as homes for their new owners; others were altered and used as barns or farm buildings. The changes in the face of the countryside were symbolic, perhaps, of changes in the spiritual landscape. The edifice of the Church as it had been known in England was crumbling as surely as the monasteries fell into ruin.

The endgame

The real engine that drove the Reformation in England was political not religious. Canon law and, more to the point, those who interpreted and enforced it had stood in the way of the king's dynastic imperatives. This was a terrible shock to a king who was used to getting his way and who expected an amenable Pope to grant his wishes without complaint. In the end, none of the arguments that he offered to the Pope made any difference at all. The Pope was not impressed by Henry's fury but may have been surprised by the lengths to which Henry was finally prepared to go to resolve the issue. The only way to secure the divorce and the succession was to overthrow the Pope in England and replace his centuries-old jurisdiction with an authority more agreeable to the king's wishes. That authority was Henry himself. As Supreme Head, Henry made the decisions of consequence and, despite the fact that he always remained true to his understanding of orthodoxy, he rather liked the power his new circumstances opened to him.

It would be a mistake, however, to see the Henrician Reformation as an exclusively political affair, for politics and religion were inextricably wedded during this period in a way which may be difficult to understand in our own pluralistic and essentially secular society. Henry and Cromwell were not entirely secular men, cynically using religious language to hide a jurisdictional revolution. The changes in the Church of England in the 1530s had spiritual as well as legal significance. To be sure, in 1536 the English Church to a large extent maintained the outward appearance it had always had, despite the fundamental changes that the government had made in law. Yet the theology of the Reformers did have an impact on this 'official' Reformation and provided much of the philosophical and theological grounding for the moves that the government made. The *Collectanea* had been instrumental in providing an ideological framework for the royal supremacy and had attacked the Roman theological edifice as well as papal supremacy. It served as a good starting-place for those who argued for a more Protestant reformation.

But because politics and religion were so intermingled, the fallout from political events could prove critical one way or the other. The year 1536 was a busy one for Thomas Cromwell. Not only did it see the beginnings of the dissolution of the monasteries and the trouble that caused, but it also saw the fall of Anne Boleyn and Cromwell's attempts to define the Church which had been created by the break with Rome. It is singular that the man most responsible for the dissemination of Protestant ideas during the early days after the break with Rome was not the archbishop of Canterbury or any other divine but Thomas Cromwell. We know little of his personal spiritual life, and one always suspects that his religious proclivities were determined more by his assessment of political reality than by any deep spiritual convictions. The fact remains, however, that the spread of Protestant ideology owed more than a little to Cromwell's position of power in the 1530s. Whatever Cromwell's personal religious feelings were, we do know that the diplomatic situation in Europe made him look to an alliance with the Lutheran princes in Germany. In 1532, English friendship with France had given Henry the confidence to go ahead with his marriage to Anne Boleyn. But European diplomacy in this period was always volatile and by 1535 France and the Empire had moved closer together. For England, at least in Cromwell's opinion, this meant a resumption of isolation unless he could forge some kind of alliance with the Lutheran princes of Germany.

Cromwell began his campaign to seek an alliance with the Lutherans as early as 1533, but it came to nothing. This was partly because of the king's reluctance to enter into any alliance (he never believed that there was any real threat to England at this time) but also because of his essential orthodoxy. For Cromwell, who felt that the threat from an alliance of Catholic nations on the continent was real, the only sensible alliance would be with the Protestant states in Germany. As a result he used his position to promote Protestant ideas and to elevate reformers to positions of authority in the Church. This would give the impression at least that England was Protestant. Cranmer, of course, was already in place. In 1535, Cromwell succeeded in having clearly identified reformers such as Hugh Latimer, Edward Foxe and Nicholas Shaxton appointed to the episcopacy. He also encouraged and supported the work of reformers such as Robert Barnes, as well as providing financial backing for major publishing projects in support of reform. It was Cromwell, for instance, who personally provided important funding for the publication of the English translation of the Bible known as the 'Matthew Bible'.

The king himself was always lukewarm towards Protestant ideas, even though he had used them while seeking his annulment. When Luther's writings first began to turn up in England, Henry had moved to refute them. He had little hesitation in rooting out heresy and punishing offenders, but the situation now demanded a different attitude. Without the superstructure of Rome, the Church in England lacked definition. What was it? What did it believe? In answer to these questions the government moved in 1536 to provide some shape and form. The Ten Articles, in July, were the work of the Convocation of Canterbury but were motivated by Cromwell. These essentially orthodox articles left the door open to Protestant interpretation, especially in the matter of the number of the sacraments. While the Articles made specific mention of baptism, penance and the Eucharist, they remained silent on confirmation, ordination, marriage and extreme unction (the last rights). As a basic text or formulary of faith, the Ten Articles were ambiguous and far from complete, but they were enforced by Cromwell's 'Injunctions' published a month later. Moderate stands were taken against images in churches and against pilgrimages, and some holy days and saints' days were proscribed. Transubstantiation was not specifically mentioned, although a fledgeling doctrine of the 'real presence' was (which, presumably, could be taken to mean any of a variety of things), and the Lutheran concept of justification by faith alone was watered down in an attempt to make it acceptable to more conservative churchmen. These articles were hardly revolutionary and, although they pointed towards reform, travelled down that road only a short way. The ambiguity was by design – consensus and unity were being sought, as was an alliance with the Lutheran states in Germany. And if the framers of the Ten Articles appeared to be walking on theological eggshells, the process was hardly reversed in 1537 when a second attempt at a formulary, the *Institution of a Christian Man* (more commonly known as the 'Bishop's Book'), made some attempt to deal with the vexed questions of purgatory, justification and the status of the four sacraments missing in the Ten Articles (now found to be somehow 'lesser sacraments').

A much greater success for the Protestants was the production of an approved vernacular version of the Bible. There had been unofficial versions of the Bible in English before. In 1407, as we saw above (p. 18), the Council of Oxford had outlawed the publication of the complete Bible in translation. Now the agitation for that policy to change had a sympathetic ear in the government. The first officially recognised version of the Bible in the vernacular appeared in 1537, when royal permission was given for the Matthew Bible to be sold. In 1538, Cromwell's Injunctions required that all churches acquire a copy. By 1540 there were editions of the Bible which were both available to and affordable by individuals. The central position of Scripture in the Protestant argument made it imperative to make the actual text available, and an official version gave the vernacular Bible the stamp of authority, even though the king's policy was far from Protestant. There were certainly those who opposed the new translation, and there is no question that many churches took their time in complying with the Injunctions. So the Protestants did not have an unmitigated success in 1539, and such success as they did have would be short-lived: it would be some time before the Bible in English was freely available.

These halting steps towards a reformed Church were a frustration to those who had a more radical agenda and certainly did little to enhance the prospects of a diplomatic entente with the Lutheran states in Germany. At the same time, conservatives were alarmed at some of the changes. Men like Stephen Gardiner saw a vast difference between support for royal supremacy and Protestantism – a distinction that was not always made by the reformers[4] – and resisted the changes that were being made by Cromwell and Cranmer.

If the situation was not pleasing to everyone, this was partly because the government needed to strike a middle ground between conservatives and radicals in order to preserve some kind of unity. The king's commitment to orthodoxy and his reluctance to commit himself wholeheartedly to a Protestant Church were further reasons for the hedging of bets in the English formularies of faith. For these reasons the crisis which struck the king's marriage in 1536 was of the utmost concern to those who supported a reformed Church. Anne Boleyn and her family, who had become increasingly important at court once she had the favour of the king, actively supported the Protestant cause. Anne used her influence and power to advance those with apparently reforming ideas – among them both Cromwell and Cranmer. Her fall could have drastic consequences for the reformers.

In the midst of the project for the dissolution of the monasteries and the redefinition of the English Church, the king's second marriage began to fall apart. When Anne Boleyn was delivered of a girl, Elizabeth, in September 1533, Henry did not hide his disappointment. When, in January 1536, another pregnancy ended in the miscarriage of a deformed foetus, the king was horrified and was easily persuaded that the child was not his. Never shy about expressing his feelings, the king was clearly displeased. The death of Catherine of Aragon in the same month further weakened Anne's position.

Anne had been very skilful in the years leading up to her marriage, but her tactics thereafter, often overbearing and tactless, had made her enemies at court. By 1536 it was evident that Anne Boleyn had overplayed her hand. As long as she could convince Henry that she would bear him the son he desired, she could hold on to power. The king, however, was beginning to doubt whether he would ever have a suitable heir by Anne Boleyn and was increasingly irritated by her attempts to manipulate him. The deformed foetus appears to have convinced the king that his second marriage, like his first, was not approved of by the Almighty. However, as long as Catherine was alive Anne's position was safe – Henry could not end his marriage to Anne without raising further questions about the validity of his first marriage. Once Catherine was dead this was no longer a problem.

When Anne fell in 1536, a serious blow might have been struck against the reformers had it not been for the fancy footwork of Thomas Cromwell. Cromwell, who had been one of Anne's faction at court, recognised the danger to reform and to himself if Anne were to fall. He knew that her enemies had a plan which included her overthrow, a restoration of Princess Mary to the succession and the marriage of Henry to Jane Seymour. They also desired the reversal of much that had changed under Cromwell. As the author of many of the changes that had been wrought in the Church and government, he was also initially identified as a target. But Cromwell acted first and quickest. Allying himself with those opposed to Anne in order to protect himself and his achievements, he accused the queen of adultery and incest. Whatever the truth of the accusations, they were enough to destroy Anne Boleyn and her party at court. She was executed on 19 May 1536. Henry married Jane Seymour only eleven days later. If there were those who thought the haste with which the king remarried undue, no one said so.

As Cromwell had been in control of the *coup d'état* against Anne, the basic policy of reform was not immediately damaged. It was after Anne's execution that the Ten Articles and the Injunctions of 1536 were issued, and it was in 1537 that the 'Bishop's Book' was published. By September 1538, Cromwell felt strong enough to issue another set of Injunctions which not only made the purchase of a Bible in English mandatory but took a strong line against images, and centres of pilgrimage. As Christopher Haigh has pointed out, many parishes managed to save their images, and compliance with the Injunctions of 1538 was hardly universal. But some of the most significant shrines in England perished at this time; most notably, the shrine of St Thomas Becket at Canterbury was destroyed.[5]

September 1538 may have been the Protestant high-water mark during the reign of Henry VIII. By November 1538 it was clear that the king was growing increasingly uncomfortable with the changes that were being made in religion by Cromwell and Cranmer. The participation of the king in the trial of John Lambert, and Lambert's subsequent execution for heresy, sent out a signal to the Protestants which was reinforced in the summer of 1539. Cromwell's enemies, led by the duke of Norfolk and Stephen Gardiner, took advantage of the king's displeasure to sow the seeds of discord between the king and his most important minister. In 1539 the Act of Six Articles returned the Church to an unambiguous orthodoxy (excluding papal supremacy) and enforced this orthodoxy with prescribed punishments. Among other things, transubstantiation and auricular confession were reaffirmed. Clerical marriage, a practice which had crept in, was condemned. Vows of chastity were held now to be inviolable (an article which caused some distress to Archbishop Thomas Cranmer, whose marriage was an open secret). Laws against heresy were now enforced with vigour in some places. Cromwell's consensus disappeared and many radicals fled to the continental Protestant strongholds in Switzerland and along the Rhine.

The political situation in Europe had been partly responsible for a more conservative policy being adopted after September 1538. Both France and the Empire were now taking significant action against Protestants, and they had agreed between themselves not to join in any alliance with England. In November 1538, the Pope sent out envoys to preach a crusade against the English, and, although with hindsight we see that there was little hope of this attracting any real interest, the English were sufficiently alarmed by this development to make preparations for invasion throughout 1539.

Cromwell's failure to deal with the crisis diplomatically ultimately meant his downfall. His efforts to secure an alliance with the Protestant states in Germany met with failure: the king was unwilling to make any religious concessions to the Lutherans. When Jane Seymour died after bearing the son that Henry wanted in October 1537, Cromwell had seen an opportunity to seal an alliance with the German Protestants through another marriage. Nothing came of this plan initially but Cromwell persisted. However, the eventual union between Henry VIII and the Protestant Anne of Cleves in January 1540 was a disaster. Henry was not pleased with this marriage either in principle or in practice. Henry's tactless reference to Anne of Cleves as a 'Flanders mare' told only part of the story. Cromwell's enemies had been busy. Throughout the winter and spring of 1540 both Norfolk and Gardiner actively worked against Cromwell. Norfolk, on a mission to France, sent back reports which seriously undermined Cromwell. Gardiner attacked indirectly by accusing Robert Barnes, a known associate of Cromwell, of heresy.

By May 1540, Cromwell's position had deteriorated significantly. He had lost the confidence of the king. Henry was unhappy with the wife that Cromwell had secured for him; an unhappiness made all the more profound when the duke of Norfolk (a man of conservative and Catholic leanings) introduced Henry to his young and seductive niece, Catherine

Howard. In addition, the reasons for the fourth marriage were rapidly disappearing. The amity between France and the Empire was breaking down and Cromwell's policy of an alliance with Protestant Germany appeared to have real drawbacks. The French were looking for new friends, and, as Norfolk pointed out, Cromwell was the man who stood in the way of any Anglo-French alliance. It also came to light in the spring of 1540 that Cromwell not only had been lax in enforcing the Act of Six Articles but was actively protecting those who did not subscribe to it. With Cromwell's enemies marshalling against him and the king wishing another divorce which would undo most of Cromwell's foreign policy, his days were numbered. Arrested under the watchful eye of Norfolk in the council chamber in June 1540, he was executed in July, having provided, as a last service to the Crown, the evidence necessary to secure the end of the king's marriage to Anne of Cleves.

Cromwell's fall from power meant that any significant moves toward a reformed Church were forced to wait until a more friendly environment towards Protestantism was created by the accession of Edward VI in 1547. To be sure, Cranmer was still archbishop of Canterbury and remained friendly with Henry VIII, who, to his credit, never turned against him. But Cranmer was isolated: the Act of Six Articles had seen the resignation of two of his allies among the bishops, Latimer and Shaxton. Always more a scholar than a politician, and although he continued throughout the remaining years of Henry's reign to work on reforms within the Church (and in particular in his own diocese of Canterbury), he was never successful in persuading either the monarch or the Convocation to take the Reformation any further than it had already come. In fact, a number of steps were taken to reverse the progress the Protestants had made. The 'Bishop's Book' was revised, emerging in 1543 as *A Necessary Doctrine and Erudition for any Christian Man*, or the 'King's Book'. This was an entirely conservative document and written in the spirit of the Act of Six Articles. The English Church was a peculiar entity – it was out of obedience with Rome but maintained what was essentially an orthodox theology and structure of belief.

This did not mean that the conservatives who had conspired to bring down Cromwell had it all their own way. The conservatives under Norfolk and Gardiner had gained influence with the king but not control over him. Henry VIII always had his own vision. Grim testimony to this vision was given soon after the execution of Cromwell in 1540, when Henry had three Protestants (including Robert Barnes) burned for heresy but also executed three 'papists' for treason. The macabre symmetry of these executions does not indicate a policy of neutrality as has sometimes been suggested.[6] While Henry could not abide heresy and punished those who deviated from his orthodoxy, he was equally insistent that those who agitated for a return to Roman obedience would be punished as well, because both were threats to the royal supremacy.

The marriage of Henry to Catherine Howard in August 1540 served as a symbol of the conservatives' influence, but only for a short time. The liveliness and youth that inspired the king to believe himself young again also led the new queen, barely more than a child herself, down the dangerous path of indiscretion. In the autumn of 1541 she was accused of adultery and executed for treason in February 1542. There appears to have been substance to the charges made against her, and the king was devastated. Norfolk and the conservative faction scrambled to dissociate themselves from her disgrace. This did not help the conservative cause.

The last years of the reign of Henry VIII were characterised by factionalism, war and religious ambiguity. The conservatives never succeeded in rooting out Thomas Cranmer, try as they might. Gardiner made a serious effort to destroy the archbishop in 1543, but the king protected his old friend. What is more, after the passing of the Act of Six Articles, it became clear that Henry himself was interested in establishing a consensus somewhere in between the Protestants and the conservatives. Throughout the latter years of his reign the pattern established in the summer of 1540 after Cromwell's fall was repeated – while Protestants were punished for violating the Act of Six Articles, papists were also executed for denying the royal supremacy. But if a policy of moderation is laudable, it also tends to send out mixed messages. English was maintained as the language in which the faith was taught, and the Lord's Prayer, the Creed and the formularies of faith were all learned in the common tongue. The English Bible was retained, but this did not mean that it was any more available to the average person (the whole point of a vernacular Bible) for access to it was severely restricted by the Act for the Advancement of True Religion in 1543. Essentially, this allowed only upper-class men and women to read the Bible (women being allowed to read it only privately, however). Keeping the interpretation of the Bible under control had always been the reason that the Church had resisted vernacular editions, and the restrictions now imposed on the English Bible would seem to be a blow against Protestantism. Yet the very same Act which limited access to the Bible also mitigated the penalties for violations of the Act of Six Articles, and by 1544 legal procedures were introduced to protect those accused of heresy in the Church courts, making it more difficult to convict.

Henry remained essentially orthodox but rejected some of the elements of medieval religion. It became clear that while he would not be shaken from his essentially orthodox beliefs, he was not opposed to reform where he felt it was needed. The fact that he did not sweep away all the changes that the Protestants had introduced may have been because he realised that there were forces at work which he could, or would, no longer control: in some areas, such as Kent, Protestantism was too strong to be rooted out.[7] On the other hand, Henry was at war with Scotland (from 1542 until the end of his reign) and with France (from 1543 to 1546), and may have seen the importance of consensus and unity at home. Whatever Henry's motives were, the result was that the conservative faction was unable utterly to defeat the Protestants but that the Protestants were kept firmly in check. Ironically, we find Henry himself, never the most tolerant of men, making a plea for forbearance in 1545 and condemning extremists on both sides of the debate.

The old order was rapidly changing in the mid-1540s, and new alliances were forged. Though Gardiner and Norfolk held on to the king's favour for a time, by the end of the reign they were no longer in a position of influence or power, partly through their own error and partly through the efforts of a revitalised Protestant faction. New, younger, men were growing in importance. Edward Seymour, earl of Hertford and uncle to the young Prince Edward, was influential not only because of his relationship to the heir to the throne but also because of his proven military ability. John Dudley, Viscount Lisle and later the infamous duke of Northumberland, was also proving himself an able commander and councillor. Both these men were ambitious, and both leaned towards the reformed religion. It is no surprise, then, to find them in alliance with Cranmer and attempting to take power from Norfolk and Gardiner. In 1544, this new Protestant faction attempted to remove Gardiner from the king's favour, but Henry protected the bishop of Winchester even as he had protected his archbishop a year earlier.

There were other worrying signs for the conservative faction. Henry's sixth wife, Catherine Parr, whom he married in 1543, appeared to have Protestant sympathies, and it was to Protestant divines belonging to Catherine's circle that the education of the heir apparent was entrusted. In response the conservatives attempted to destroy the Protestant faction in a vigorous persecution under the Act of Six Articles in the spring of 1546. Those arrested included both Latimer and Shaxton, but attempts to link Catherine Parr to heretical beliefs failed. Nevertheless, the conservatives were in a strong position and managed to undermine the Protestants further by having Protestant books banned and burned.

Despite the strength of the conservative position, there was one thing that they did not have: control of the heir to the throne. By the autumn of 1546, it was apparent that Henry's health was rapidly failing. The heir to the throne was under age, and a regency government would be necessary. Both sides realised that control of Edward would be crucial to their political survival. In the faction fighting that took place from the autumn of 1546 until Henry's death at the end of January 1547, it was Hertford who emerged as a clear winner. Taking advantage of his position as uncle to the heir, Hertford was able to place himself near the king. Strong political alliances with members of the king's Privy Council allowed him to outmanoeuvre his conservative rivals and exclude them from power after the king died. Gardiner fell out of favour because he was reluctant to exchange some of his lands with the king. But it was Hertford's allies who conducted the negotiations and they may have misrepresented the deal both to the bishop and to the king. Norfolk spent the last part of the reign in the Tower with the threat of execution hanging over his head after his attempts to secure control of the regency were interpreted as treason. Hertford and his allies had successfully removed the leaders of the conservative faction from play. When Henry died in the early hours of 28 January 1547, it was the new men who were at his bedside and who controlled, and may have altered, the king's will. Gardiner, Norfolk and most of the conservative faction were effectively excluded from power in the next reign. Had the old king wished otherwise, he was no longer in a position to do anything about it.

To his own way of thinking, Henry had always remained orthodox in his religious beliefs. Apart from the exclusion of papal jurisdiction and supremacy in the Church, the theological changes that were made were not staggering. The disappearance of the monasteries and some other religious foundations certainly altered the appearance of the Church and seriously undermined its wealth, but there was no such shift to a Protestant theology as was characteristic of the Reformation on the continent. The Church of England that Henry left behind may have been schismatic but it was not Protestant. But more radical change was certainly in the wind. By the end of Henry's reign the stars that were rising were all inclined towards Protestantism and they would be the most influential voices on the council of the boy king Edward.

The Reformation at the grassroots

If the political situation by the end of the reign was complicated, the religious situation was ambiguous. The Protestants, who had been on the retreat since the fall of Cromwell, now had a government which was sympathetic but an ecclesiastical edifice that was orthodox. Although they were in a strong position to take over the administration of the Church and effect the changes that they thought necessary, there remains a serious question as to the strength of the support that the Protestants had at the grassroots. Were the people of England ready and willing to be Protestants, or were they content with orthodoxy?

There is no clear answer. It is difficult to assess the extent to which Protestant ideas made any headway in England during the reign of Henry VIII. Part of the difficulty we have in assessing what the people believed is a lack of evidence. Some of the evidence that we do have is fragmentary, often anecdotal, while other evidence needs to be treated with caution. The way men and women made out their wills, for instance, can sometimes indicate their religious feelings, but the surviving wills from the end of the reign of Henry VIII do not give us an unequivocal picture of how influential Protestantism was among those who wrote them. In addition, we are never really sure just whose views a will reflects – does it reflect the faith of the dying person or the views of the one (usually a priest) who copied it down? It is very difficult to draw any solid conclusions from such problematical evidence.

If we look into the reigns of Edward and Mary, we do find that some aspects of the Protestant reforms during the reign of Henry VIII must have had an impact on the lives of ordinary people. A man in Gloucester was familiar enough with the Bible to defend his multiple marriages with Old Testament texts, while the number of humble men and women able to cite Scripture accurately to their examiners during the Marian persecutions indicates that the English translation of the Bible was read and learned by more than the educated and the clergy. On the other hand, we find that some aspects of the Protestant programme for reform were not so successful. Pluralism continued to be a problem (as did non-residence), and the ignorance of the clergy continued to be noted. The reforming bishop John Hooper's visitation of the diocese of Gloucester in 1551 revealed a number of pluralists and non-residents, at least one case of simony, and ten clergy who could not even recite the Lord's Prayer – surely the most basic of requirements for a priest. Some twenty years after the anticlerical debates in the Reformation Parliament, these problems still existed.

It seems clear, however, that by the end of Henry's reign Protestantism had made some gains. Some areas in England were more receptive to Protestant ideas than others: Protestantism appears to have been strong in the south and the east, while the north and west were conservative. This broad generalisation takes into account the closer contacts that the south and the east had with the continent but is useful only if we take into account the notable exceptions. While the counties of Essex and Kent were receptive to Protestantism, Sussex and Hampshire were strongly conservative. Lancashire was generally conservative, but northern cities such as Hull and Leeds are now known to have had important Protestant communities. Even here we must speak in general terms, for all communities, whether counties or villages, were divided on religious issues to some degree or another. The picture is further complicated when one considers that there is often a correlation between religious belief and social or economic divisions and disputes – as we have seen, the Pilgrimage of Grace was not simply a religious uprising but involved a number of other factors.[8]

The advance of Protestantism in England during the reign of Henry VIII, then, was patchy. Some areas accepted it with alacrity, while others resisted. This pattern continued into the reign of Edward VI, when efforts to recapture ground lost to the conservatives during the last years of Henry's reign and to expand the extent of the reform met with stiff resistance on the ground in some areas. Indeed, it is hard to see the Reformation in England as secure until well into the reign of Elizabeth. In 1547, the Church had seen some reforms but was far from being 'reformed' in any sense meaningful to Protestants. Protestant ideas were abroad but as yet represented only a minority opinion. But when Henry VIII died those who controlled Edward VI were either Protestant or sympathetic to Protestantism, and they controlled the destiny of the English Church.

Notes

Introduction

1 M. Powicke, *The Reformation in England* (Oxford, 1941), p. 1; J. Foxe, *The Acts and Monuments of the Christian Church*, ed. G. Townsend (London, 1843–9), vol. V, p. 697.
2 There is neither time nor space in this format to go into any depth in discussing the various approaches to the Reformation which have been taken by historians. Sometimes the differences are extremely subtle and beyond the scope of an introductory text. I stress the very general nature of my remarks here and urge students who are interested in the historiography of the period to consult the following texts: C. Haigh, 'The recent historiography of the English Reformation', in C. Haigh (ed.), *The English Reformation Revised* (Cambridge, 1987), pp. 19–33; and R. O'Day, *The Debate on the English Reformation* (London, 1986).
3 C. Haigh, *English Reformations* (Oxford, 1993), p. 14.

1 Why a Reformation?

1 The term was first used in relation to the 'protest' of the German Protestant princes when they formed the defensive organisation known as the Schmalkaldic League.

2 J. Guy, *Tudor England* (Oxford, 1988), p. 122.
3 Erasmus, born in Rotterdam and living in England for a time, was the guiding light of north European humanism. His witty, subtle but biting criticisms of the Church were an influence on reformers and orthodox churchmen alike.
4 G. R. Elton, *England under the Tudors* (London, 1974), p. 112.
5 The Avignon Papacy lasted from 1309 until 1377.
6 The period 1378–1417 is known as the Great Schism. During this forty-year period there were a number of popes and 'anti-popes'. Things got particularly complicated towards the end of the Schism with a pope in Avignon, one in Rome and a third in Pisa.
7 Guy, pp. 26–7.
8 J. F. Davis, *Heresy and Reformation in the South-East of England* (London, 1983), p. 5; Haigh, *English Reformations*, pp. 25–39.
9 Winter was also ordained while under age – another abuse sometimes cited by reformers.
10 Haigh, *English Reformations*, pp. 25–8.

2 The 'King's Great Matter'

1 It should always be remembered that the annulment was not referred to as a divorce at the time. There should be no misunderstanding on this point. In the sixteenth century, apart from the views of a very few advanced thinkers (such as the reformer Martin Bucer), the concept of divorce did not exist as it does today. While one might admit in the twentieth century that a marriage had in fact taken place and was now, for one reason or another, ended, in the sixteenth century nothing of the kind would be accepted. There might be any number of reasons to dissolve a marriage. If the marriage was never consummated, for instance, this might be sufficient grounds for annulment, as in the case of Emperor Maximilian I and Anne of Brittany. If that could not be claimed, it was necessary to show that there was some good reason why a lawful marriage had never really taken place. It would be claimed that, outward appearances to the contrary aside, the participants had been knowingly

or unknowingly living in a state of sin, and no marital state had ever existed.
2 G. R. Elton, *Reform and Reformation* (Cambridge, 1977), p. 103.
3 Henry was related to all of his wives. Anne Boleyn, for instance, was a seventh cousin and traced a common blood-tie back to Edward I.
4 The reasons for this outburst are obscure. It may very well have been part of a diplomatic ploy by Henry VII to squeeze further concessions out of Ferdinand of Spain. Prince Henry never seems to have had any doubt about the desirability of a marriage to Catherine at this time.
5 Leviticus xviii. 16 and xx.21.
6 Deuteronomy xxv.5.
7 Guy, p. 82.
8 He was appointed dean of both Hereford and Lincoln cathedrals.
9 E. W. Ives, *Anne Boleyn* (Oxford, 1986), pp. 141–50.

3 The break with Rome

1 Guy, p. 126.
2 Ibid., p. 125.
3 S. Lehmberg, *The Reformation Parliament* (Cambridge, 1970), p. 3.
4 Haigh, *English Reformations*, pp. 94–6.
5 Guy, p. 126.
6 £100,000 from the Convocation of Canterbury, and £18,000 from the Convocation of York.
7 This is the argument of Elton, first articulated in his *The Tudor Revolution in Government* (Cambridge, 1953).
8 Guy, pp. 154–64.
9 Lehmberg, p. 132.
10 Ibid., pp. 137–8.

4 The progress of the Reformation

1 Guy, p. 144.
2 Elton, *England under the Tudors*, p. 144.
3 Ibid., p. 145.

4 Robert Barnes, when executed in 1540 for heresy, failed to see this distinction.

5 Haigh, *English Reformations*, pp. 152–67.

6 Elton, *England under the Tudors*, p. 194.

7 Guy, p. 195.

8 See D. M. Palliser, 'Popular Reactions to the Reformation during the Years of Uncertainty 1530–1570', in F. Heal and R. O'Day (eds), *Church and Society in England: Henry VIII to James I* (London, 1977), pp. 35–56; and W. J. Shiels, *The English Reformation 1530–1570* (London, 1989), pp. 68–78.

Further reading

There are innumerable books of worth written on the Reformation in the time of Henry VIII. I have listed just a few here that may be of help to those wishing to pursue the subject further.

Collinson, P. *Godly People: Essays on English Protestantism and Puritanism*. London, 1983. An excellent account of the progress of Reformation and its development in the sixteenth century.

Collinson, P. *The Religion of Protestants*. Oxford, 1982. A very good book describing what the Protestants believed, although it concentrates on the Elizabethan period.

Cross, C. *Church and People, 1450–1660*. London, 1976. A good general introduction.

Dickens, A. G. *The English Reformation*. London, 1964. A landmark. While many of Dickens's conclusions have been shown to be inaccurate, there is much here of worth when studying this period.

Duffy, E. *The Stripping of the Altars*. New Haven, Conn., 1992. A complicated and detailed account of the changes in the Church from the late fifteenth century through the Reformation. Not for beginners.

Elton, G. R. *England under the Tudors*, second edition. London, 1974. The classic textbook on the period. Somewhat out of date now, but much of his argument is still debated.

Elton, G. R. *Reform and Reformation: England, 1509–1558.* London, 1977. Detailed but readable; an important discussion of the period.

Elton, G. R. *Reform and Renewal: Thomas Cromwell and the Common Weal.* Cambridge, 1973.

Elton, G. R. *Policy and Police: The Enforcement of the Reformation in the Age of Thomas Cromwell.* Cambridge, 1972. Perhaps Elton's most important book. If the student is interested in how the Reformation was enforced, this is the book to read.

Guy, J. A. *The Public Career of Thomas More.* Brighton, 1980. One of the better biographies of More.

Guy, J. A. *Tudor England.* Oxford, 1988.

Haigh, C. *English Reformations.* Oxford, 1993. A revisionist view of the Reformation. There are some problems with Haigh's arguments, but this is a very useful book, and students should take note of it.

Haigh, C., ed. *The English Reformation Revised.* Cambridge, 1987. A good collection of essays; they are detailed and scholarly but very useful.

Heal, F. and O'Day, R., eds. *Church and Society in England: Henry VIII to James I.* London, 1977. Another useful collection of essays.

Heal, F. and O'Day, R., eds. *Princes and Paupers in the English Church 1500–1800.* Leicester, 1981.

Heath, P. *The English Parish Clergy on the Eve of the Reformation.* London, 1969. A scholarly study of the state of the Church just before the Reformation.

Ives, E. W. *Anne Boleyn.* Oxford, 1986. Everything you always wanted to know about Anne Boleyn – a good read.

Lehmberg, S. E. *The Reformation Parliament, 1529–1536.* Cambridge, 1970. 'The' work on the Reformation Parliament. It is detailed and scholarly but accessible.

Lehmberg, S. E. *The Later Parliaments of the Reign of Henry VIII.* Cambridge, 1980.

Marius, R. *Thomas More.* New York, 1984. Another biography of More.

McConica, J. K. *English Humanists and Reformation Politics under Henry VIII and Edward VI.* Oxford, 1965. A much-maligned look at English humanism. Flawed but still useful.

81

Muller, J. A. *Stephen Gardiner and the Tudor Reaction*. New York, 1926. The best book on Stephen Gardiner.

Palmer, M. D. *Henry VIII*. London, 1971. A study guide: very worthwhile.

Parmiter, G. *The King's Great Matter*. London, 1967.

Pollard, A. F. *Wolsey*. London, 1929. Dated but still to be recommended.

Rex, R. *Henry VIII and the English Reformation*. London, 1993. A study guide with a Catholic point of view.

Ridley, J. *Thomas Cranmer*. Oxford, 1962.

Scarisbrick, J. J. *Henry VIII*. London, 1968. Groundbreaking study of Henry VIII. Thorough, scholarly and important.

Scarisbrick, J. J. *The Reformation and the English People*. London, 1984. A broad look at the Reformation.

Shiels, W. J. *The English Reformation 1530–1570*. London, 1989 Another study guide, and a very good one.

Wilkie, W. E. *The Cardinal Protectors of England: Rome and the Tudors before the Reformation*. Cambridge, 1974. A scholarly book on pre-Reformation relations between England and Rome.

Youings, J. *The Dissolution of the Monasteries*. London, 1971. An important account of the dissolution, but not for a student new to the period.